WHITE-COLLAR UNIONISM

T. STRANGLEMAN,
23/12/93,
COLCHESTER.

CAMBRIDGE STUDIES IN SOCIOLOGY

Editors: R. M. Blackburn and K. Prandy

This series presents research findings of theoretical significance on subjects of social importance. It allows a wide variety of topics and approaches, though central themes are provided by economic life and social stratification. The format ranges from monographs reporting specific research to sets of original research papers on a common theme. The series is edited in Cambridge and contains books arising mainly from work carried out there. However, suitable books, wherever they originate, are included.

Published

R. M. Blackburn and Michael Mann
THE WORKING CLASS IN THE LABOUR MARKET

K. Prandy, A. Stewart and R. M. Blackburn
WHITE-COLLAR UNIONISM

K. Prandy, A. Stewart and R. M. Blackburn
WHITE-COLLAR WORK

A. Stewart, K. Prandy and R. M. Blackburn
SOCIAL STRATIFICATION AND OCCUPATIONS

Also by K. Prandy

PROFESSIONAL EMPLOYEES

Also by R. M. Blackburn

UNION CHARACTER AND SOCIAL CLASS
PERCEPTIONS OF WORK (*with H. Beynon*)

White-Collar Unionism

K. Prandy, A. Stewart
and R. M. Blackburn

First published 1983 by
THE MACMILLAN PRESS LTD
London and Basingstoke
Companies and representatives
throughout the world

ISBN 0 333 32889 2 (hardcover)
ISBN 0 333 32890 6 (paperback)

Printed in Hong Kong

Contents

v

List of Tables and Figures

TABLES

FIGURES

Preface

The study reported in this book arises out of the same project as our previous *White-Collar Work*. It is part of the sociological research programme of the Department of Applied Economics in the University of Cambridge. The original project was financed by the Social Science Research Council, whose support we should like to acknowledge with gratitude.

Survey research is ultimately made possible by the willing co-operation of those who are interviewed, and so our major thanks must go to the many whose responses constitute the greater part of this work. We should also like to thank those responsible in the employing establishments – of which there are rather too many to be named individually – who gave not only their permission for the interviews to be carried out, but also their time and help in other ways. Similarly our thanks go to the staffs of the trade unions and other representative bodies who completed the questionnaires locally or through our earlier postal survey.

Large-scale research is also a team effort, and the authors reporting the results depend very substantially on the support provided by many others. We extend our thanks in general terms to all those who helped make the research and its reporting possible: the interviewers who collected the data, those who helped work on it by offering their statistical and computing skills, and those who provided typing, secretarial and general administrative services.

We should also like to thank John Holmwood for his valuable comments on the earlier draft versions of the book.

1 Trade Unionism and Social Class

In this, the second of our books focused on non-manual employees, we are concerned with collective representation and particularly with employee involvement therein. Our major aim is to locate unionism in a broader theoretical context, and thus to address significant issues of social stratification. This means continuing a long-running debate which we now seek to bring up to date. In the process we hope to develop a more adequate understanding of both trade unionism and stratification.

In the previous volume reporting the results of our study of non-manual workers (Prandy, Stewart and Blackburn, 1982), we were concerned with presenting a model which related individuals' responses to their experience within a system of distribution of rewards, on the one hand, to the ways in which such responses contributed to the maintenance of or change in the system, on the other. In the concluding chapter we argued that a model of this kind could be related to the concerns of traditional class analysis. However such analysis has tended to separate issues of maintenance and change and to pursue each, mistakenly in our view, in terms of evaluations rather than cognitions. The failure of class analysis to provide an adequate account of either maintenance or change can in large part be associated with this orientation, as can the identification of maintenance and change as separate problems. We have discussed these issues at some length in our previous work including the companion volume. There we indicated that since this present volume was to deal very largely with actual union involvement, rather than desires as in the previous work, a fuller discussion of the nature of trade unionism, and its relationship to traditional class analysis could be deferred to this point.

It is particularly appropriate to look at these questions in the context of a study of non-manual workers because, as we shall see, much of the more recent discussion of trade unionism has been in relation to its growth amongst the 'middle class'. Thus the debate has often been part of a more general one concerned with the idea of the 'middle class', and

1

hence necessarily with the whole theory of class or of social stratification. Obviously, however, the nature of unionism for manual workers has to be considered, not simply because one issue in the debate is the meaningfulness of separating (at least some sectors of) non-manual workers from the manual, but more importantly because the question of the nature of trade unionism as such has generally been pursued in terms of manual unionism.

The classical theories of trade unionism have all taken it more or less for granted that the phenomenon they deal with is specific to the manual working class. Thus, even if only in a very limited sense, the 'class' nature of trade unions has seemed unproblematic. This agreement upon aspects of trade unionism is not fortuitous. As we shall see it is based upon certain shared assumptions, within apparently disparate theories, about the nature and organisation of work experience, even though at first sight the differences between theories seem more important than their similarities. Thus, in the Marxist tradition, whilst unions are clearly seen as organs of class struggle, their economistic concerns (which reflect the ways in which they operate to dampen class polarisation) and lack of revolutionary commitment are taken to indicate their limited class nature. In the liberal tradition class has been viewed more in terms of the stratification of social groups, and unions have been seen as forms of representing and pursuing more or less extensive sectional interests within a system of mutual dependence.

However, what they share is a conception of class as based upon the market position of labour in the production of commodities, and of trade unionism as the pursuit, however limited, of class interests. With this in common it is not surprising that they should agree that trade unionism is, typically, a condition of manual employees, since these are the people most unequivocally associated with the direct sale of labour in the market. (We shall outline a little later the problems and equivocations in dealing with white-collar employees.) We wish to challenge both the relationship of trade unionism to *market* mechanisms and the identification of stratification in modern societies as a 'class' phenomenon in this sense, though we agree that it is closely tied to social inequality. We shall argue that, especially among non-manual employees, trade unionism is strongly established in areas such as government employment where conventional market models cannot be applied and that such areas of employment cannot be accounted for as substantively dependent upon the operation of the market sector. However, as a prelude to more detailed discussion of these issues, and as a means of setting them in context, we shall return to recent discussions of the nature of trade unionism in general and white-collar trade unionism in particular.

In a book which moved against the tide of opinion that trade unionism is a 'class' phenomenon, Bain, Coates and Ellis (1973) carried the argument to the opposition. Their position owes a great deal, as they acknowledge, to the work of Flanders (1970) who believed that unions had made, at best, only modest economic gains for their members. In what has become something of an industrial relations orthodoxy he argues that the primary purpose of unions is a concern with job regulation. He believes that they are less involved in collective bargaining than in the negotiation of collective rules through a diplomatic use of power. Thus the major value of a union to its members is in its capacity to protect their dignity. As Fox (1975) shows in his critique of this position, it is based on a false distinction between the 'economic', governed by impersonal market forces, and the social or political. That is, Flanders argues that the effectiveness of trade unions in the former sphere is necessarily limited, and since their method of collective bargaining (or, rather, negotiation) places them in the latter, it is clearly there that they operate.

This attempted separation of the economic from the social is criticised by Fox, as it has been in more general terms by ourselves in other work including the earlier, companion volume to this one. However for the present we shall not develop that position, but rather draw out one of the particular implications of Flanders' argument. In accepting the claims that unions have had little economic impact, either as regards their own members or as regards labour as a whole, the Flanders approach tends to play down the 'class' element in unionism. If unions have not secured greater returns for the working class *vis-à-vis* capital, and if economic issues are anyway not the most salient, then clearly they should not be regarded as in any sense class organisations. This is the kind of argument put by Bain, Coates and Ellis.

Although its title, *Social Stratification and Trade Unionism*, is general, their book in fact deals primarily with white-collar trade unionism. Moreover it has very little to offer in the way of positive analysis, but concentrates instead on attacking those studies which argue or assume that there is a link between social stratification and trade unionism. The authors' way of doing this is to show that no hypothesis of a simple cause and effect kind, taken just on its own, will in all cases be supported by the evidence. However, at some points they accept and use previously rejected arguments to demonstrate the invalidity of other hypotheses. So, for example, having earlier devoted their energies to rejecting a relation between unionism and class consciousness or class position, they later quote evidence of unionateness to indicate *class* rather than *status* ideology, and also evidence of white-collar workers who are outside unions not for status reasons but because they do not need them – apparently because of their favourable class position. In the process they frequently employ the twin tactics of, on the one hand using an author they are attacking to make their own point for them, with the author 'having to admit' or 'being forced to conclude', and on the other, of misusing quotations to make quite different, even opposite, points. Thus, for example, one of the present authors is described as being 'at some pains to maintain the distinction between *professional associations* and trade unions', but 'is forced to conclude that although *unions* among professional workers are different from those among manual workers, "the similarities are nevertheless greater than the differences"' (p. 78; our emphasis).

In general they argue that since attempts at job regulation occur among groups other than working-class ones and since such attempts are not necessarily associated with subsequent identification with the working class, then trade unionism is not in essence a class phenomenon. Certainly the emphasis in Flanders' work on job regulation reflects an important element in the activities of unions which makes them comparable to other kinds of occupational associations, such as professional bodies. However, at the same time, this emphasis diverts attention away from the fact that this is just one aspect of *market* regulation. It leads to the position where all forms of regulation of the supply of labour are treated as comparable, but as distinct from other forms of regulation of markets. At the same time their view of the issue primarily in market terms prevents them from taking account of broader social processes of inequality.

As Adam Smith pointed out, the motivation for individuals in a similar market relation to conspire amongst themselves to modify the workings of the 'hidden hand' is very strong. The degree of commitment to 'market forces', especially where they involve being at a financial disadvantage or, perhaps more importantly, being subjected to un-certainty, is far from widespread. Groups similarly placed in the market will seek to maintain as high as possible a degree of predictability and, if possible, advantage. Since there are numerous areas in which either those involved, as buyers or sellers, or third parties such as the state, believe it necessary to regulate the 'free' operation of the market, any such moves often find support.

Clearly there is a sense in which all forms of market regulation by the participants share a similarity by being just that. On the other hand, they can all be distinguished from one another on the basis of the nature of the market concerned and the position within it of those attempting its regulation. In that it recognises the distinctiveness of the market for labour, the job regulation approach implicitly accepts this point while also denying it. It is both more limited and potentially more fruitful than the orthodox economic view in which unions are seen as a form of cartel acting as monopolists in the sale of certain types of labour. Whether such monopolies can be maintained, and a higher market price gained for that labour, is seen as a matter of empirical investigation, though the pressure of competition is normally taken as making it unlikely except perhaps in a few special cases.

This orthodox economic view explicitly treats labour as a commodity; the job regulation approach, which is not inconsistent with it, does so implicitly, in that it attempts to relegate the commodity aspects of labour to a separate 'economic' sphere and concentrates on the special social or political element – that it involves people holding 'jobs'. However, whereas the former sees all labour as simply another kind of product, the latter fails to recognise that the separation of labour and product is a specific, not a universal feature of production. Thus, although the implications are in some respects different, each view treats the capitalist commodity form as the norm. In so doing they each fail to provide an adequate account even of the market sector. More seriously, they cannot set market processes within a broader social context, particularly one in which there is a significant non-market sector.

The difficulties can be illustrated by considering the treatment of professional associations by Bain *et al.* As we shall see, this leads on to fundamental issues. In line with their general position, that all forms of job regulation are essentially similar, they argue that professional associations are 'the craft unions of a different social group'. Although they specifically refer only to employed professionals they make no distinctions as to the form of employment, and make their general points – in accordance with their view of regulation – as if all forms of professional association, at least of the qualifying and occupational types, were identical. Thus they ignore the very different market situations typically involved. However, the classic, and in terms of protection of their members the most successful, examples of professional associations are those of private, fee-paid practitioners. For these it is misleading to place an emphasis on *job* regulation and to ignore the fact that there is also involved the regulation of the conditions of sale of the product, as for example in setting fees as a proportion of certain other costs. This may not always be immediately apparent because the product is often in the form of an intangible 'service', where the labour is indistinguishable from the product. Often this is simply a result of the fact that the product is not produced under the conditions of capitalist commodity production, with its separation of the two, formally under the special conditions of the employment relationship, and substantively by means of division of labour and so on.

In the case of professional associations of this kind it is at least as plausible to argue that they are a form of producer cartel as that they are similar to unions. The reason that they are able to operate successfully as such is that they are a relatively small number of sellers facing a large number of buyers. The market situation of craft workers may at one time have been similarly advantageous, especially with the carry-over of elements of pre-capitalist relations with, for example, a similar difficulty of separating the labour from the product. However the fact of employment has made it difficult, if not in most cases impossible, for craft unions to exercise the same kind of unilateral regulation. Inevitably, job regulation in their case, but even more in that of non-skilled workers, has necessitated collective bargaining, where the interests of the two sides are to a large extent opposed.

Apart from independent practitioners, the term 'professional' is usually applied to highly qualified employees with specific skills. While such groups exist in the private sector, the degree of collective organisation is weak, and in recent times new professions have been typically concerned with the provision of non-commodity resources organised directly by the state (for example, town planners and social workers). The ability of such groups to pursue unilateral job regulation is limited by the fact that they face, virtually, a single employer and one that is, in the case of the central government, often directly involved in the provision of the necessary training facilities. Some degree of regulation of entry, of definition of competence and of the forms of relation with other groups is nevertheless a possibility. However it occurs largely through 'political' processes and is not mediated through market regulation. Here the state is involved directly as employer; it purchases labour and controls the disposal of the product, but the product does not occur in a commodity form. It is either uniquely provided for general social benefit or is given as welfare outside a relationship of direct exchange.

Thus professions are far from homogeneous with respect to the conditions under which their members are employed. What these two major types have in common and what distinguishes them from many groups of unionised workers is that their labour is not provided under the conditions of capitalist commodity production. However, both forms are dependent upon expanding industrial production and upon state activity; the provision either of employment directly, as in the second case, or of legal protection and sanctions, as in the first. In other words the processes which give rise to 'commodity production' also give rise to other relations between labour and product involving centralised intervention in the free market for products in the name of the public good.

The discussion of professions raises an issue which is of far wider significance: that of the relation of market to other more general social processes. The importance of differences in market conditions has to be recognised; equally, though, it is necessary to appreciate that divisions within markets are intrinsic to an understanding of their nature and the processes by which they have arisen – issues which usually lie outside conventional economic analysis. Any attempt to simplify these issues by ignoring the distinctions fails to confront the basic nature of the system of inequality. It is a strength of class models of stratification, especially the Marxist one, that they are able to specify the conditions of the growth of class interests in the development of industrial societies. However, central to Marx's theory is the belief that commodity production was such a forceful and successful form of economic activity that eventually it would displace, temporarily, but more or less completely, all other forms of activity – i.e. a capitalist mode of production would hold sway until undermined by the contradictions inherent in it. Class interests in such circumstances are clearly located within a market model.

Non-market aspects of industrial development were not anticipated by Marx as part of capitalist societies. Indeed, he cites the weakness of the traditional professions (church and army) in the face of capitalist commodity production as evidence of the imminent pervasiveness of wage labour. He seems to have greatly underestimated the requirements in an industrial system for employment in the area of circulation (rather than production) of commodities and in the area of reproduction of labour. It is in these areas that the services of independent professionals were required and flourished. In addition many features of social organisation seem to indicate that developing industrial societies were never so careless of social benefits, as opposed to individual interests, as his theory of capitalism implied.

Attempts by later writers to modify Marx's model to deal with its most obvious limitations have generally accepted the centrality of markets while giving modified statements of their constitution. Weber, for example, accepted that class was a phenomenon of market location, but argued that market relations were more diverse than Marx had allowed. In particular he discounted the similarity of labour under capitalism. He argued that different kinds of labour had different interests in the market and that these interests might be in competition. There is not a single working class but, potentially, as many classes as interest groups in the market. In other words, while he accepts wage labour for capitalists in a system of commodity production as the central phenomenon of capitalism, he sees the divisions among wage labourers as more important than the circumstance in common.

He also added non-class forms of social stratification to his analysis, but as we have argued elsewhere (Stewart, Prandy, and Blackburn, 1980 especially chs 1 and 4; Holmwood and Stewart, 1981) the relationship between class and other factors is specified in an inadequate and contradictory manner. In any case he did not believe that these other factors affected his analysis of class.

Recent neo-Weberian writings have maintained the emphasis on markets in their discussions of Western countries (Parkin, 1979; Giddens, 1973), as have many recent writings within the Marxist tradition. Braverman (1974) can be distinguished from most other Marxist writers in maintaining that the Marxist model operates in industrial societies more or less in the form specified by Marx. He believes that the degradation of labour has been effectively accomplished, though the authorities hide the fact by the manipulation of employment statistics. However, most Marxists accept that polarisation has not occurred in this way and seek to incorporate a 'middle class' into the basic model. They argue that a greater or lesser proportion of non-manual employees belong neither exclusively in the proletariat nor in the bourgeoisie (e.g. see Poulantzas, 1973; Carchedi, 1977; Wright, 1976; Crompton and Gubbay, 1977). They have something of the circumstances of proletarians, but perform some of the functions of capital. They are thus a 'middle class' in that they straddle each. Once again we have been critical of the form of analysis (Stewart *et al.*, 1980, ch. 10; Holmwood and Stewart, 1981), but at present we merely wish to draw attention to the way in which it seeks to maintain the basic model of class specified in relation to capitalist commodity production.

We believe that all of these theories are too limited in their approach to inequality. We do not believe that commodity production is the defining characteristic of modern industrial societies nor that areas of economic activity outside commodity production can be explained by subsumption under capitalist models, as is often attempted, or by the specification of a secondary role in their relationship to the commodity sector.

The state, it must be recognised, is a major employer of labour, and over the longer term is becoming increasingly so. Work in the public sector is carried on by employees – wage earners – so while it is possible to agree that separation of labour and product is a central feature of industrial societies, this separation is achieved in processes other than a dominant system of commodity production. Being employed, selling one's labour divorced from its product, is not a sufficient condition of proletarian status in any of the major theories of social class. Classes are defined, at a minimum, in terms of market relationships, and within the fully developed Marxist model in terms of a specific relationship of exploitation. Government employees are difficult to place in such systems. The absence of a market for their product means that other forms of economic determination of the distribution of their services, and of the levels of their incomes, are necessary. They are not in a 'Marxist' situation of proletarian exploitation.

In various attempts to modify the basic theory to deal with the state it is seen as a mechanism for the maintenance of capitalism. In that case state employees have an interest in identifying with the capitalist function. Yet government employees are the most highly unionised of non-manual workers. Does this mean that their form of unionism is a conservative accommodation to the status quo? We do not believe that it is. We believe that a great deal of state provision is progressive in the sense of extending social resources and ameliorating the conditions of the disadvantaged. These have been legitimate objectives of 'class' organisations including trade unions and, we shall argue, they are related to the challenge trade unionism presents to market criteria of distribution by its emphasis on more universalistic, egalitarian criteria.

As we pointed out when discussing professional associations, the state has an influence upon forms of social and economic organisation other than as a direct employer. In the last two decades this type of influence has become increasingly prominent in this country as successive governments have attempted to have some form of incomes policy accepted in both the public and private sectors. On occasions there is a rhetoric of free market forces, but the conception of the economy as a totality is not of independent producers united by the 'hidden hand' of market forces. Rather it is of interdependent sectors of the economy whose relationships must be managed by centralised policies. One consequence of recent government policies, especially those concerned with the limitation of increases in incomes, has been to create common interests across all forms of employment which can override great differences in employment conditions. In the private sector it has also created situations where employer and employee are united in their opposition to the government's attempt to limit the income of the latter.

CLASS CONSCIOUSNESS AND CLASS IDENTIFICATION

The sociological approach to trade unionism has been much concerned with the issue of class consciousness. To an extent this is probably a consequence of its development in relation to the growth of unionism among white-collar workers where the nature of consciousness is an obvious problem. Bain *et al.* describe the basic model, or at least the more 'sophisticated' version, as one in which 'the workers' position in the social stratification system generates a certain picture or image of industry and the wider society which shapes their attitudes to trade unionism' (1973, p. 9). One can sympathise with these writers in their attempt to create a coherent picture from a number of diverse studies and commentaries. Indeed, they have tried to be fair, by presenting this model with the intervening variable of social imagery as one which is superior to that which omits it on the assumption 'that the causal mechanism of the relationship is so self-evident that it need not be spelt out' (p. 8). Unfortunately, it is not the case for many of the writers whom they discuss that 'social imagery' has been introduced in such a way. It is a less, not a more, sophisticated sociological approach which deems it necessary to introduce an intervening variable of subjective consciousness to 'explain' a relationship. This is essentially a commonsense view, and not one which lays stress on convincing explanations as being ones where relations are embedded in satisfactory theories.

It is to the nature of such theories that those who wish to deny the link between trade unionism and social stratification should address themselves. If they were to do so, they would find that the writers they criticise – including, we must point out, two of the present authors – do not fall into the errors of which they are accused, but that they have not in truth been wholly convincing in their theoretical formulation. In relation to the first, the point to note is that the writers criticised are usually well aware that, in Lockwood's (1958) terms, 'there is no inevitable connection between unionization and class consciousness'. Lockwood argues that 'concerted action is a function of the recognition by the members of the occupational group that they have interests in common; class consciousness entails the further realization that certain of these interests are also shared by other groups of employees', but he goes on to say that 'the trade-union movement is a working-class movement, and to the extent that clerical workers become involved in trade unionism they have to come to terms with its wider class character' (p. 137).

This degree of ambivalence is also found in those writers who seek to build upon Lockwood's work. Blackburn (1967) most explicitly recognises the variable nature of unionisation, not only in respect of membership completeness, but also in terms of unionateness of character. Nonetheless, although at the extreme it may be very slight, 'it is an important feature of unionisation that it may be taken as an index of class consciousness' (p. 9). Similarly Prandy (1965), accepting Lockwood's point above, says that it 'should not be overstressed'; for him, all unions express 'consciousness of conflict of interest', and only in extreme form, not necessarily manifest even by most manual worker unions, does it reach full class consciousness. Thus none of these writers unequivocally equates class consciousness and trade unionism. On the other hand, they are convinced of a general connection, but one which is based upon an explicit assumption that the trade union movement is 'the main vehicle of working-class consciousness', and that 'to study the class consciousness of the clerk is to study the factors affecting his sense of identification with, or alienation from, the working class' (Lockwood, 1958, p. 13). However, only by initially assuming that the trade union movement is a vehicle of class consciousness can they then use unionisation, in particular that of non-manual workers, as an index of class identification. This involves strong implicit assumptions of social classes based upon conventional understandings of manual workers as proletarians. Unless the class nature of the trade union movement can be given a firmer theoretical foundation, to allow that even manual unions fall short of full class consciousness gives ammunition to the critics when they question the initial assumption of the class nature of trade unionism.

At this point, indeed, Bain *et al.* seek to strengthen their argument in typical manner by calling on a different tradition for support. Having made their general attack on the idea of a link between social stratification and trade unionism, they then accuse Blackburn and Lockwood, specifically, of adopting 'a particular position in a long standing debate between Marxist and non-Marxist scholars on the nature of capitalism and on the character and historical potential of the working class and its organisations' (p. 101). No such charge can be levied against those making it! For them it is apparently possible to adopt a position which is both non-Marxist and Marxist at the same time. Since there can be little doubt of Marx's views on the nature of unions as reflecting or expressing class relationships, whatever reservations Lenin and others may have had about their revolutionary potential, it is, to say the least, odd for those who deny any connection with class to enlist Marx in order to criticise other writers for their restricted interpretation of class consciousness.

However, if we set aside the source of the criticism, there is some justification in the claim that those in the 'sociological tradition' of the study of white-collar unionism 'have not made clear exactly what they mean by class consciousness', and thus have not provided a satisfactory link with trade unionism. Part of the problem has been that whereas in the Marxist tradition variations in class consciousness occur serially, the studies in question wish to examine variations at points in time. Class consciousness on the Marxist model develops as capitalism develops and its contradictions and limitations become apparent. The common interests which underlie it depend upon common relations to the means of production involving common circumstances of expropriation. It thus involves more than a sense of identity with the wider labour movement in that such identity develops around specific interests and reaches its culmination when the limitations inherent in the formal relations of capitalist production are revealed. In those circumstances there will be a 'conception of an *alternative* society, a goal towards which one moves through the struggle with the opponent' which Mann (1973, p. 13) argues is an indispensable element of true revolutionary consciousness.

Lockwood and Blackburn are concerned with current variations of consciousness within the working population, and in the context of British society, the specific reference of their studies, their choice of indicators of class consciousness is perfectly understandable. It is not that they are 'suggesting that class consciousness should be defined within a social democratic frame of reference' (Bain *et al.*, 1973, p. 101), as if this were the only way in which it could be defined, but simply that this is the frame of reference in which the British labour movement has, in any significant way, acted. Though they set their arguments within a traditional class model, their approach has elements which are amenable to another form of class analysis which accepts employment status as a basis of common interests without tying it directly to expropriation and the polarisation of classes.

In essence they are providing criteria for different levels of commitment to general interests of employees, and as we have argued employee status is not tied to capitalist relations of production as is generally supposed. Both individuals and organisations differ in the extent to which specific interests are pursued in preference to general interests. This is also affected by circumstances, so that at different times there are different relations between them. Class consciousness varies, therefore, not in terms of an approach to revolution within the development of capitalism, but in terms of the particularity or generality of interests (from those organised on a personal basis, through organisation of specific groups of employees, to general movements of employees). Among employees the greatest commitment to general as opposed to specific interests are likely to be found among lower groups (though not the lowest – see Prandy, 1979) with least personal advantages and least ability to mobilise particular resources in their own interests. Within such a view class action, we shall argue, has radical consequences, but not those of a proletarian revolution.

Of course, the British situation is not identically repeated in any other country, and anyone undertaking a study of trade union membership elsewhere would have to take account of the particular social and historical context. In all cases we would expect some relationship to action in the general interest of employees, but how one would develop a set of indicators of class consciousness would obviously depend on which society was being studied. However one would also have to take account of our earlier point about the theoretical framework within which the concept was used. For example, it would probably be generally agreed that on the usual Marxist definition the largest French union, the CGT, or even the next-largest, the CFDT, takes up a more explicitly class-conscious stance than any British union, and that this is represented in the views of its members (see Gallie, 1978). On the other hand it would be difficult to credit the French unions with any great achievements on behalf of the working class. Union membership is, overall, relatively low (about 32 per cent, less in the private sector), and their effectiveness as bargaining agents, that is in gaining benefits for their members through industrial action, is very limited. As Gallie's study shows, even in a situation of relatively strong support, the French trade unions 'were unable to bring sufficient pressure to bear on management to enforce any major changes in an institutional system that had substantial costs in terms of the workers' experience of employment' (p. 316). It is true, of course, that the unions were largely unconcerned with any such changes, preferring a perception of 'their role as one of *mobilizing* the work force for a far reaching structural transformation of society' (p. 239), and avoiding the dangers of co-optation. However, this necessarily implies a degree of failure in one of the CGT's aims, the 'daily struggle . . . to limit, to act as a brake on the effects of capitalist exploitation' (see p. 240), while there is no evidence for any compensatory gains in the political sphere. Those who wish may continue to believe in the greater likelihood of the revolutionary transformation of French than of, say, British or Swedish society, despite the declining political fortune of the French Communist Party, but in the meantime France remains a society with a highly unequal distribution of income and a tax system which, if anything, operates in a regressive manner. In so far as recent political developments may serve to change this pattern, it appears that they will do so more within a 'social democratic' than a 'revolutionary' frame of reference.

In certain respects there is a parallel between this situation and that regarding enterprise unionateness which we discussed in our previous volume. There we pointed out that the behaviour of a representative organisation, particularly the sanctions which it brought to bear, was dependent upon the behaviour of other parties, most obviously the employer. Thus greater militancy could well reflect employer opposition, and so indicate relative failure rather than success. Consequently, we argued that we had to consider not the actual sanctions most frequently employed, but those which it was clear a particular organisation was prepared to use if necessary. This was possible because such a prospect did fall within the range of experience of most bodies, either their actual experience or what they could see as possible experience, based either upon their own history or upon the situations of other, similarly placed organisations. Since class consciousness is necessarily more all-encompassing, taking in both actual and realistically conceivable experience, the parallel breaks down and we have no direct clues as to how, say, British workers would react to the overthrow of the existing system of collective bargaining. However, we can argue from inter-societal comparison, and note Mann's comment that 'the refusal of French and Italian employers to co-operate with trade unions in "their" factories has always been observed to be a very potent encouragement to Communism among the workers' (1973, p. 42). There is no great desire on their part to incorporate the working class, apparently.

In our view the French example shows very clearly that greater class consciousness, in the sense usually understood, is not associated with greater working-class success, except possibly in a negative direction. The faithful may continue to believe in the greater potential, but their theoretical grounds for doing so are open to serious doubt. For, as Mann asks, 'if working-class consciousness varies inversely with the degree of capitalist maturity in a whole society, what are we to make of orthodox Marxism?' (p. 43). Certainly there may be greater instability in societies where employers have not acted in the way that capitalists should according to the pure model, but the chances for a successful proletarian revolution seem uncertain. On the other hand since, for Marx, the maturity of capitalism implies the more probable imminence of socialism, how is this to be squared with the apparently low degree of class consciousness?

One answer to this question we shall develop in this chapter. That is, that what we need to be concerned with are the practical effects of consciousness. Just as in Banks' (1970) study 'the search for evidence of class consciousness amongst steel workers was directed away from verbal manifestations of attitude per se and towards overt expression of class unity in concrete behaviour, such as support for the General Strike' (p. 205), so we believe it necessary to look at the effects of unionism with respect to employment relations. Like him we shall look for evidence that trade unionism can fruitfully be understood as revolutionary activity though not, as in his case, 'on the basis of converting the *theoretical concept*, "revolution", into an *empirical term* devoid of all traces of violence' (our emphases), but by embedding the concept within a different theoretical framework – which is what we believe he also does.

However, as we shall see, this treatment of aggregate class action appears to bear little relationship to individual consciousness, in the usual sense. We have elsewhere (Prandy, 1979) suggested an approach to individual class consciousness which stresses, not evaluation, but cognition and the role that experience plays in its development. Although we have not the space here, we believe this could be elaborated, so that what becomes central is not knowledge of an alternative form of society as something distinct from and theoretically unintegrated with current conditions, but an understanding of existing society which sees it in terms other than those of capitalism. In so far as class action modifies 'capitalism' and the principles upon which it claims to be based, so experience is actually transformed, and understanding with it.

Our view, then, is that to study trade unionism within what Bain *et al.* describe as a 'social democratic' framework is necessary in the British situation, since change occurs not through an expression of revolution-ary zeal, but through the solution of immediate problems and the transformation of existing practices. Contrary to their 'common sense' view, it also makes more theoretical sense, in terms of class conscious-ness, than using a more revolutionary framework.

THE ECONOMIC CONSEQUENCES OF TRADE UNIONISM

The economic effects of trade unionism have been extensively discussed, though seldom using realistic models of social and economic processes. Perhaps greatest attention has been paid to the issue of whether or not unions produce real economic advantages for their members *vis-à-vis* non-members. Studies in the USA, where unionisation is less extensive than in Britain, are generally regarded as demonstrating that any gains of unionised over non-unionised labour are relatively slight, of the order of 6 per cent (Lewis, 1963), but some would put it higher. In Britain, where union membership is more widespread, one might expect any gains from unionisation to be correspondingly more difficult to realise, but in fact some estimates put it as high as 40 per cent (Mulvey, 1978). The studies in this area all assume that the effect is one way, from unionism to relative wages, whereas there is a view, represented by dual labour market theory (Doeringer and Piore, 1971), that it is high-paying sectors which are more likely to be unionised. However the standard view tends to be supported by the evidence that over time increases in unionisation are associated with higher increases in earnings, at least in the interwar period (Burkitt, 1975). As a means of pursuing sectional interest, then, unions may be considered at least moderately successful. The greater problem arises in trying to determine whether, in what respects, and how, they go beyond the representation of sectional interests towards the representation of more general class interests.

The empirical economic studies of the kind that we have already referred to appear to be in fairly full agreement that if the object of trade unionism has been class conscious in the limited sense of securing a redistribution from capital to labour then it has failed. In Mulvey's (1978) words, 'unions probably have no appreciable influence on the long-run distribution of factor incomes' – that is, the returns to labour and capital. Even so, others have disputed the claim, in particular by including salaries together with wages in labour's share (Glyn and Sutcliffe, 1972). However, if this point is inconclusive and pecuniary returns have stayed constant, the rise and growth of trade unionism has certainly been associated with an improvement in the non-pecuniary aspects of employment. Partly this has been achieved by the actions of unions in establishing minimum or model standards, but partly by legislation which may not necessarily result from union pressure. Both represent interesting forms of the intrusion of 'non-market' criteria. For reasons of ignorance and perhaps of a degree of non-commensurability between individuals, competition for labour between employers is likely to be even less on non-pecuniary factors (Blackburn and Mann, 1979) than it is on wages, that is to say, probably very limited (Reddaway, 1959; but cf. Wilkinson, 1962).

The value of studies of distribution between capital and labour, dealing as they do only with issues internal to the market sector, is very limited. They ignore the development of the public sector and the social provision of wealth generated within it. As a consequence they leave out of their analysis a major element of redistribution and a major source of interest in that redistribution – employment in the public sector. We shall return shortly to the relationship between trade unionism and the production of social resources.

In so far as trade unions are organised on the basis of occupational or industrial groupings, then necessarily the interests they pursue are sectional ones. Indeed, even a general union, open to almost any group of workers, will, almost by definition, improve the lot only of its members, perhaps even to the detriment of non-members not covered by its agreements. Many people would regard the trade unions in the United States as generally being of this kind, that is pursuing various sectional interests in a 'business' fashion, without any very developed conception of class interests. Significantly, whatever the strength of particular unions, that of the labour movement overall, for example in terms of membership, is weak, and this raises interesting questions about class consciousness within a national context. We may argue that the general level of class consciousness is low and that this is reflected in the weakness of the trade union movement. However, this brings us back to the question of whether union membership can be used as an indicator of class experience at the individual, as distinct from the societal, level, that is whether union members experience other than purely sectional gains.

A clue to the answer is, we believe, contained in data on the way unions affect differentials among those they represent. Here there is general agreement that in both the USA and Britain 'unions have apparently been successful in reducing interpersonal wage differentials' and 'have been inclined to reduce geographical, industrial and inter-firm wage differentials' (Mulvey, 1978, pp. 115–16), and that 'they narrow wage differentials between individuals and firms, while contributing to a secular process of smaller inter-area differentials' (Burkitt, 1975, pp. 125–6).

Within the unionised sector, therefore, union members are to an extent freed from the vagaries of the 'free' market determination of earnings. Instead, though again only to a degree, more egalitarian criteria are pursued, and results achieved. Thus even in a situation of limited union organisation, it is possible to substitute more universalistic, egalitarian and class-orientated determinants of income differentials for those of the market. The pursuit of sectional interests, that is to say, is not necessarily inconsistent with a degree of class consciousness, at least in the sense of solidarity over earnings. Again it is a difficult question to answer, within the bounds of a single society over a relatively short time period, whether such class consciousness would expand beyond the groups defined by membership of particular unions to embrace a wider working class. However, comparative evidence is valuable in suggesting an answer, and we are naturally led to look at the consequences of more extensive unionisation.

The question we need to consider is whether more extensive unionisation is associated with the development of non-market criteria effecting a more egalitarian reward distribution. Although there are technical difficulties in evaluating the relevant processes there are two forms of comparative evidence to help suggest an answer. The first is historical, where we can consider the relation between changes in the extent of unionisation and pay differentials. Although, in the case of Britain for example, it is difficult to establish any precise relationship between these two, it is quite clear that the two major periods of both rapid increase in union membership and notable decline in pay differentials occurred at the same time – around the two world wars. Thus total union membership rose from 17.9 per cent in 1911 to 37.6 per cent in 1921, and from 29.9 per cent in 1938 to 45.1 per cent in 1948 (Bain, 1967, p. 14), while according to Routh (1980), in the period 1914–20 'there was a general narrowing of differentials. Money earnings of manual workers increased rapidly, while non-manual earnings lagged behind'; and in the period 1934–44 'manual earnings moved up at accelerating pace, with maximum rise between 1938 and 1940. Salaries regained their pre-depression level somewhat later (1936 or 1937) and, by 1940, had failed to improve on it' (pp. 178–9). 'In subsequent years [to 1955], there were fluctuations about the 1940 relationship and no further radical changes' (p. 156).

In so far as Routh's comments relate only to manual/non-manual differentials they are not particularly apposite to our argument. That is, such changes could be attributed to the gains of unionised over non-unionised workers, rather than to developments within the unionised sector, which is our main concern. It may be argued that the gains in union membership and in income were both results of changed market conditions. However if workers are more ready to support unionism in favourable market circumstances it suggests they are less afraid to oppose employers and they see possibilities of achievement. Thus, whether or not the gains of manual workers are attributable to unionism, the processes are not insignificant in terms of class relations. However, for the present the issue is whether they achieved greater equality of rewards. It is important, therefore, to note that similar egalitarian tendencies were operating within the manual working class. Thus the pay of the unskilled men relative to skilled men rose from 60 per cent in 1913–14 to 71 per cent in 1922–4 and, after falling back to 66 per cent in 1935–6 (during a period of declining union membership), to 70 per cent in 1955–6 (Routh, 1980, p. 124). As Routh notes, for the first period 'the final outcome . . . was a radical improvement in the relative pay of the unskilled' (p. 137), and for the second 'what is still more curious is that rates for the unskilled should generally have risen more than those for skilled workers, for . . . unemployment was much heavier amongst the former' (p. 158). Similarly, Turner (1957) has little doubt that 'in Britain the narrowing of differentials has been associated with periods of rapidly rising wages, and particularly with the growth of mass trades unionism'. He sees the major cause as being the unions' preference, reflecting the predominance of unskilled workers, for flat-rate increases. Moreover, there is evidence (King, 1972) that other forms of differential, those between regions, were also reduced by the increase in union strength in the period 1914–20.

We must beware of simply accepting such evidence at its face value. Over the whole period the structure of employment was changing, so that the distribution and content of work defined as skilled or unskilled was not the same at the different dates. Nevertheless, the net effect has been a more equal distribution and the timing of the changes, often occurring in relatively limited time periods, is significant. With regard to narrowing regional differences, it might be argued that this was simply an extension of market forces (more perfect knowledge), except that to a large extent jobs in different regions are not really equivalent and labour is not particularly mobile. In any case union action must be seen as attempting to effect change through the modification of existing 'market' relations.

Presumably because of the still widespread attachment to theories of price determination by the interaction of supply and demand (despite the very poor support given them by empirical studies of income determination), Burkitt (1975) claims that 'most economists argue that unions contributed little to the narrowing of occupational differentials, since it took place even in countries where unions were weak' (p. 119). Unfortunately, historical evidence for other countries is not easily available, which makes doubly interesting the other kind of comparative analysis that we can use to consider the consequences of extensive unionisation, that is cross-sectional studies of a number of countries. Again there are considerable technical difficulties, but the one study that looks specifically at the effects of unionisation on income distribution before tax gives a very clear indication that across the nine industrial societies considered the relationship is a strong one, with unionisation explaining around 50 per cent of the variance in income inequality (Stephens, 1979, see p. 105).

Restricting ourselves solely to the effects of extensive unionisation in the industrial sphere, those arising mainly out of the process of collective bargaining, we must conclude that there is certainly no diminution, and more probably an increase in the egalitarian tendencies which seem inherent in trade union activity. However, in looking at the relationship between unionism and class action we cannot restrict ourselves in that way, and it is necessary to consider the wider political implications of increased unionisation. Whilst we cannot go into this question very deeply or extensively, there are a number of studies which are directly relevant for even our fairly limited aim. For example, even in the case of the United States, which we referred to earlier as an instance of weak unionisation, where there have developed no formal links between the trade union movement and a particular political party, the evidence suggests that there is nonetheless a relationship between differences in the strength of organised labour in the various states and the extent of redistribution through taxation and welfare policies (Hicks *et al.*, 1978).

In other industrialised societies, of course, there have been much closer links between the trade union movement and a political party representing the labour movement. Stephens (1979) presents data showing the close association between labour organisation and such factors as the votes going to socialist parties, the years of government by socialist parties, various measures of income inequality and welfare spending. His results and those, for example, of Hewitt (1977) and Peters (1974) provide clear evidence for the effect of social democratic governments in bringing about redistribution through welfare state spending. Where other parties have pursued such policies in government, almost always to a far more limited extent, this appears to be a response to the strength of the union movement. These studies indicate that the influence of factors such as economic growth and income per head, while not negligible, are not as all-important as they were formerly claimed to be.

Thus we believe that there can be little doubt about the significance of the trade union movement in relation to the more equal distribution of material and other related benefits. Both directly through industrial action and indirectly through its effect on political policy, it has had an egalitarian influence. Not all would agree that this represents class action, especially, as some of the gains of industrial workers and of those relatively disadvantaged who, all would agree, are outside the sphere of direct capitalist production, have been at the relative expense not of capital, but of the more advantaged income earners. A full appreciation of the issues of this argument requires a thorough re-examination of the Marxist concept of surplus value – a task that we hope to carry out elsewhere, but as we argued in our previous volume the processes involved represent a considerable modification and supercession of market criteria in critical areas, undermining central elements in the conceptual structure of capitalist society in both Marxist and non-Marxist perspectives.

However, a point about the meaning of individual union membership remains to be settled. We have argued that both historically and across societies greater unionisation has been linked to greater class action. Given this relationship at the aggregate level, what can be concluded about the connection at the individual level between union membership and class consciousness? Obviously, not everyone who joins a trade union exhibits class consciousness, even of a mild degree – some, for example, may be more or less obliged to join – but equally, in aggregate terms each new member tends to make a marginal contribution to the labour movement's pursuit of class action. As was suggested earlier we cannot consider individual decisions to join or remain a member of a union outside of the historical and cultural context in which the decision takes place. 'Membership of a union' cannot necessarily be equated in different contexts, in the sense that we could argue that an American trade unionist would commit himself to the achievements of the Swedish labour movement, or a British member in the 1930s to the gains of the 1960s. On the other hand, comparative analyses show that as change occurs and unionisation becomes more extensive, so also does commitment to the current achievements and possible future progress. This is not to suggest that all members adequately understand the processes in which they are involved or that such processes are simple aggregations of individual actions. Organisational and political circumstances, in the general sense, mediate between individual workers and overall outcomes, but the general trend remains for individual action in the form of union membership to initiate and reproduce change in the system.

WHITE-COLLAR UNIONS

The question of the meaning of membership returns the discussion specifically to white-collar trade unionism. It could be argued that the growth of a wider union movement typically depends upon its extension from the more skilled, more advantaged members of the working class to the less skilled and less advantaged. Thus the egalitarian processes we have noted might be said to reflect simply the increasing ability of such groups to pursue their interests, even perhaps against the opposition of the more skilled – an opposition weakened, some would say, by the degradation of their skills. On this argument, white-collar unions represent the sectional interests of relatively advantaged groups, eager to maintain or extend, rather than to diminish existing inequalities. They are thus different kinds of organisations, membership of which has a quite different meaning.

One answer to this, of course, is that this possibility has usually been recognised. Blackburn (1967) deals most explicitly with the concept of union character, making use of previous work, particularly that of Lockwood (1958). Our own work (Prandy, Stewart and Blackburn, 1974) made explicit the distinction between enterprise and society unionateness, separating the question of the degree of militancy that would be contemplated in collective bargaining from that of the extent of identification with the wider labour movement. Much of this chapter can be seen, in one sense, as arguing that there is a strong link between these two which increases as unionisation proceeds. The importance of the link is that identification then becomes not simply a question of expressing a sense of solidarity or awareness of common interests, but is the basis of significant class action. However if white-collar unions and their members do not demonstrate any degree of identification, then clearly their role in the labour movement becomes problematic. Similarly, any extension of unionisation based on this sector would not have the kinds of consequences that we have discussed.

In fact our finding, reported in the previous volume, *was* that it was equally true that among white-collar workers enterprise and society unionateness were well related, each serving to reinforce the other. More generally there is a trend in Britain (Crewe *et al.*, 1977) and, for example, Sweden (Korpi, 1978) of increasing support for the labour-inclined party on the part of non-manual workers, and evidence that this is related to union membership (Butler and Stokes, 1969, ch. 7). More convincingly, Dunleavy (1980) draws out the inter-relationships of social class, or grade, unionisation and sectoral employment. Non-manual employees in the public sector are very highly unionised and this spills over into support for the Labour Party. (He suggests that this applies equally to controllers of labour, though in our study the higher-status occupational groups, managers and professionals, showed a greater decrease over other groups in society unionateness than in enterprise unionateness.)

It appears that public sector employees, who are difficult to locate in traditional class theories, are both highly organised and conscious of shared interests with other employees. Of course, they have a basis of interest in publicly provided services over and above their role as consumers or potential consumers of them. The provision of these services is for many of them the basis of their employment. To the extent that this provision represents gains for general social interests, public sector employees will tend to identify with economic and political organisations dedicated to such gains.

In any event, it would appear that identification with the wider labour movement and support for its policies has developed among unionised white-collar workers. Whatever may have been their attitudes tradition-ally, many groups of non-manual workers seem now to be moving closer to manual trade unionists. As to possible future developments, what is important is the historical and cultural context; the conditions under which a large proportion of non-manual groups would become unionised would represent a substantial change from the present, with correspondingly different understandings of employment relations. In so far as such a change would be in circumstances relating to social class – and it is difficult to imagine that this would not be to a significant degree – then one would anticipate similar changes in society unionate-ness. In this respect the situation is parallel to the one we have already considered in looking at the consequences, or concomitants, of extensive unionisation.

One point to bear in mind, in fact, is the part played by the growth of white-collar unions in that process. Figures given by Bain (1967) suggest that non-manual workers constituted only about 3 per cent of all union workers in 1920; by 1948 this had increased to 21 per cent, and by 1964 to

26 per cent. Similarly, in Sweden the increase in union density among white-collar workers, from 50 per cent in 1950 to 70 per cent in 1975, would have made them a considerably greater proportion of all unionised workers.

There is unfortunately very little evidence on whether white-collar unions also exhibit the internal tendencies we have noted for unions generally, that is to say, for more egalitarian criteria to be given weight as against those of the market. Certainly employers fear that this is the case. As Bain (1967, p. 79) puts it: 'Of all the "dire consequences" of staff unionism which employers predict will occur, none fills them with greater dismay than the alleged tendency of unions to introduce practices which will promote mediocrity and stifle ambition'. 'A more common theme of this argument is that white-collar unions will introduce practices which will prevent the employer from treating his staff employees on their merits as individuals.' How far such fears are justified is difficult to tell; one study (Roberts, Loveridge and Gennard, 1972, p. 187) shows that the spread of earnings is greater amongst the more highly unionised groups of technicians, but it does not consider separately situations where there is or is not collective bargaining.

The changing pattern of differentials in the public sector could profitably be analysed in relation to more general movements. There are problems in so far as civil service pay was formally determined by reference to comparability with outside groups between 1956 and 1981, although other factors such as maintaining real incomes also became involved in bargaining. To some extent, also, there may have been an influence in later years from public sector pay to that of the private sector (Elliott and Fallick, 1981). However, there can be little doubt that over the longer term the top echelons, certainly, of the civil service have lost out to the clerical officers, most notably in the 1913–24 period, but also in that of 1936–55 (see Routh, 1980, pp. 73–92). Both groups seem to have done much less well than those in the private sector. For example, between 1913 and 1924 administrative civil servants fell behind other managers with comparable incomes at the first date (Routh: compare table 2.11 and the table on p. 75), and seem to have continued to do so into the post-war period (see the figures for bank managers on pp. 77–8). Equally, civil service clerks have fared less well than bank clerks and clerical workers in general (see his tables 2.16 and 2.17). However the decline in the latter case appears to have been rather less. More recent salary movements in the public sector are discussed by Elliott and Fallick (1981), and they show a further narrowing of the differential up to 1975 (though with an increase in the 1950–69 period).

Less inequality in the public as against the private sector has also been noted in the USA (Fogel and Lewin, 1974), but unfortunately its relationship to unionisation was not examined.

If we must leave a slight question mark over the issue of the consequences for differentials of collective bargaining by white-collar unions, we think there is less doubt about their relationship to the wider labour movement. A number of unions have long been affiliated to the TUC, while others have become so more recently, sometimes after many years of contentious discussion. It may well be the case that affiliation became less contentious for white-collar unions as others joined the TUC and modified its character. By the same process the association between the TUC and the Labour Party became less clear, because fewer of the non-manual unions were prepared to take this further step or, if they did, found that a substantial proportion of their membership contracted out of the political levy. Nevertheless, TUC affiliation does represent the greater solidarity of the labour movement, and at the least imposes upon the different unions some obligation to seek a common view on many issues. Even in Sweden, where there is a separate Central Organisation of Salaried Employees, it is argued that collaboration between it and the manual Confederation of Swedish Trade Unions 'has become more and more intimate in recent years' (Ahrne, Himmelstrand and Lundberg, 1978). Similarly Korpi (1978) claims that 'in recent years the unions have also been acting more and more as one coalition of wage-earners rather than as internally competing interest groups. The increasing stress in white-collar as well as blue-collar unions on a "solidaristic wage policy", giving priority to wage increases for the lowest-paid employees, is further indication that in Sweden the competition between wage-earners is now gradually being abolished' (p. 103).

We are aware that the continuation of such unity is a matter of political debate, and that there may be a reaction against the trend. However arguments from political changes which may be short-term, reflecting particular sets of circumstances, have to be treated with caution. Longer-run trends are more important, but necessarily can be determined only long after the event. Since the significance of the place of non-manual unions in the labour movement as a whole is a comparatively recent development, there are inevitably many unanswered questions. We have argued that the class nature of trade unionism is in general quite clear; it constitutes a relatively successful form of class action. Apart from the question of income distribution, we would agree with Banks (1970) that there have been other 'permanent encroachments upon the untrammelled right of capitalist employers', although we are less sure than he is that these have led to 'the eventual displacement of capitalism by another type of social system' (p. 205). We believe that capitalism as understood by Marxist or neo-classical writers was never the dominant form of social organisation.

Such evidence as is available suggests to us that many white-collar unions play a similar role in the extension of unionisation to that of manual unions. Thus their identification with the wider labour movement constitutes participation in the form of class action that is represented by that movement. However, our analysis of attitudes and behaviour at the individual level, whilst it in part depends upon the arguments made in this chapter – which justify treating unionateness and union involvement as aspects of class consciousness – is also designed to supplement it. In the concluding chapter of the previous volume we showed how our analysis fitted in to a more general analysis of class; in this work we shall follow that up by looking specifically at involvement in unions and other representative bodies.

2 The Individual and Collective Representation

In this chapter we shall be considering the extent of involvement in bodies providing collective representation, and the individual characteristics that are associated with such involvement. This extends the analysis at the individual level that we developed in the companion volume to this one. There we dealt with the question of collective representation only in terms of the individual's perceived need for an organisation with a particular level of enterprise and society unionateness. The meaning of these concepts, and the way that they were measured, is fully discussed in the previous volume, but broadly the first, enterprise unionateness, covers the level of independence of, and militancy towards, an employer while the second, society unionateness, deals with the degree of identification with the wider labour movement. In either case the concept applies both to the actions undertaken by organisations (or, more properly, actions that they are prepared to undertake) and to the desire for such actions on the part of individuals.

For the present we are remaining at the level of analysis of individual characteristics, but there is one contextual factor that has to be taken account of from the outset. Although we collected information from establishments in the public sector which was designed, as far as possible, to give comparability with that obtained from private employers, we decided that a single analysis incorporating both sectors would be unsatisfactory. There are fundamental differences in 'market' relations, forms of organisation and relationships between employer and employees which mean that for most purposes it is preferable to treat each separately. In consequence, the bulk of our analysis, starting with this chapter, relates solely to the private sector, where there is to be found by far the greater amount of variability. Public employment will be dealt with by itself, though with some comparative reference back to the private sector, in Chapter 6.

AGREEMENT WITH REPRESENTATION

Our analysis of involvement in representative bodies is confined, in part by necessity, to those who agree with some form of representation, and it is therefore useful to begin by considering this. Agreement was determined as part of the process of measuring enterprise unionateness, simply by recording those statements relating to the latter that the individual agreed with. Necessarily, therefore, all those who disagree with all forms of representation are scored zero on the enterprise unionateness scale. The number in each occupational group who agree with representation are shown in Table 2.1. Only a minority, 268 out of 1561 respondents (17 per cent) disagree with representation of any kind, but as we would expect the higher-status groups, particularly professionals and managers, are much less in favour. Taken together these two groups are two-and-a-half times more likely than the rest to want no representation (gamma = 0.53).

TABLE 2.1   *Agreement with representation by occupation*

Occupational group	Disagree	Agree	Per cent agree
Security	2	14	88
Supervisors	23	222	91
Clerks	59	433	88
Draughtsmen	4	69	95
Technicians	52	272	84
Professionals	57	155	73
Managers	71	128	64
Total	268	1293	83

In examining the characteristics of individuals who agree with representation, the method that we shall use is that of discriminant analysis. This is essentially a means of choosing from among a set of continuous variables those which are best at placing respondents into one of a number of known categories. An indication of the relative contribution made by each variable to the classification is given by the standardised discriminant function coefficient. The sign of the coefficient indicates whether the contribution is in a 'positive' direction, which in this case is taken to be towards membership of the group of those who agree with representation, or a 'negative' one (those who disagree). The coefficients also provide a means of estimating to which of the groups each respondent belongs, and by comparing these estimates with individuals' actual group membership we gain an idea of how successful the whole set of variables is in allocating respondents to the correct category. Since we started with the assumption that membership of either group was equally probable, we would expect 50 per cent of each group to be correctly allocated by chance. We could have started with probabilities corresponding to the relative size of the groups, thereby improving overall allocation by chance, but reducing the contribution from the discriminant function and involving a poor prediction for the smaller group.

The procedure that we shall adopt in carrying out the analysis is to follow through the operation of various factors in the order corresponding to the model that we developed in our previous volume. That is, we shall begin with various aspects of social background, then in turn introduce current rewards and job characteristics, the expectations that individuals have regarding various rewards, the degree of satisfaction that they express with different aspects of their job, and finally a number of factors that were previously presented as outcomes of or adaptations to the individual's situation. Although we shall elaborate each of these categories to some extent, for full details of measurement it will be necessary to refer to the previous volume.

Background factors are taken to include all those which are prior to the individual's current situation. Among them are the father's occupational status, various aspects of the individual's educational experience, his age, the status of his first job, first job in his present firm, and length of service in that company. Not all of these (or of the variables in the sets which are introduced later) are necessarily significant for discrimination purposes when taken in conjunction with other factors. Our selection of significant variables is based on a hierarchical procedure in which the best discriminator is taken first, and subsequent ones added according to their additional discriminating power.

The first column of Table 2.2 shows which of the background factors are important. Only four are needed, in fact, to enable us to allocate nearly two-thirds of all respondents (as compared with 50 per cent by chance). The major single one is the status of the first job in the firm, such that the higher this is the more likely it is that the individual will disagree with representation. There are similar effects from both the father's occupational status and the number of years beyond the minimum that the respondent stayed on at school. Clearly, then, it is those with a less advantaged upbringing and educational career who are more disposed

TABLE 2.2   *Agreement with representation: discriminant analysis*

	Background factors only	Including social location	Including expectations and satisfactions	Including outcomes
Variables: discriminant function coefficients				
Father's status	0.28	0.22	0.19	–
Years at school	0.27	–	–	–
Part-time (day) FE	– 0.31	– 0.25	– 0.24	– 0.23
Part-time (evening) FE	–	– 0.24	– 0.23	– 0.25
Years of service	–	– 0.31	– 0.28	–
First job in firm status	0.74	–	–	–
Present job status	——	0.46	0.45	0.38
Income		0.46	0.41	0.26
Promotion perceptions		0.18	–	–
Control		0.29	0.31	–
Security: top manager	–	–	–	0.15
Promotion expectations	——		–	– 0.21
Intrinsic job expectations			– 0.17	–
Satisfaction with status			0.25	0.21
Society unionateness			——	– 0.66
Group centroids: co-ordinates				
Disagree	0.51	0.73	0.77	0.96
Agree	– 0.10	– 0.15	– 0.15	– 0.19
Correctly predicted: per cent				
Disagree	54	62	63	73
Agree	68	72	73	71
Total	66	70	71	72

towards favouring representation. In fact, this is even more apparent if we omit the first job in the firm (and first job, by which it is replaced) from the analysis on the grounds that it is too close to being an indicator of current position. Then, it is the number of years spent in full-time further education which is the best single discriminator. However, as may be seen from the table, the more time that the individual has spent in part-time day education courses, the more likely it is that he will agree with representation.

The next set of factors introduced are those relating to what we refer to as social location. They cover the respondent's present job and the rewards that are associated with it. Some of the latter, such as income, are directly measured, but most are the individual's perceptions – of such aspects of his job, for example, as the extent to which he is able to use his abilities, the degree of control he has, his status within the company and his promotion prospects (or achievements). Several of the perceptions are explicitly relative; for example, security is assessed by comparison with an average top manager or manual worker. Similarly, we have the respondent's assessment of the earnings of these same people within his company.

When these variables are introduced into the analysis there is an improvement in the prediction of group membership to 70 per cent correct overall. Although the difference is less marked than when background alone was considered, there is still a tendency for there to be more correct predictions for those who agree with representation than for those who disagree. Disagreement is more likely among those in higher-status jobs, with higher earnings, more favourable perceptions of their promotion prospects and a greater sense of being able to exercise control in their jobs. It also remains the case that it is more likely on the part of those with higher-status fathers, although the effect weakens slightly. On the other hand, once these variables relating to current situation are brought in, the status of the first job in the firm ceases to be significant. This is true also of the number of years at school beyond the minimum, but not of time spent in part-time day education. In fact, the other measure of part-time education, that relating to evening courses, now shows a similar effect. Those more likely to agree with representation tend to be those who have spent longer in either of the part-time forms of education. As the column shows, they tend also to be those with longer service in the firm.

The third set of factors, expectations and satisfactions, are largely self-explanatory. They cover the same set of rewards that were included amongst perceptions, except that there is only one measure of expectations of intrinsic job rewards (not control and use of abilities separately) and of security (not top manager and manual worker separately). Also, in the case of earnings we have figures of what the respondent believes people at his own level, top managers and manual workers ought to earn. Expectations were originally introduced into our model to be offset against social location factors, as well as to reflect social background and experience. Satisfaction was seen, in part, as a resolution of perceptions and expectations, but also itself as a reflection of aspects of experience more broadly.

Including expectations and satisfactions makes a slight improvement to overall prediction. For the most part the effect of variables introduced earlier does not change, apart from being a little weaker. The exception is that expectations of promotion replace the perceptions. The only other new information is that those with higher expectations regarding the intrinsic aspects of their work (bearing in mind that perceptions, at least of control, are being allowed for) are more likely to favour representation, while those who are more satisfied with their status tend to disagree with it.

Finally, the outcome factors are introduced. These were seen as forms of adaptation by individuals to their situation. One, attitude to top management in the company, is largely attitudinal, but the others are intended to tap predispositions to action. They are self-estrangement, or psychological withdrawal, which we see as a form of the use of the self as an object in the work situation without full involvement, job attachment – inversely, the propensity to leave the job, either permanently or temporarily – and the two aspects of unionateness already referred to.

In fact we do not include enterprise unionateness in this analysis because all those who disagreed with representation were necessarily scored zero on that variable. Of the remainder in this set only society unionateness is significant, but it emerges as easily the best discriminator. For the first time there is slightly better prediction of those who disagree than of those who agree. The general pattern of other influences remains, though most become weaker, indicating that they tend, in conjunction, to be associated with society unionateness. Those best associated, the father's occupational status and years of service in the firm, cease to have any significant separate effect. Thus, in summary, the picture that we are left with is that allowing for the fact that those expressing a greater degree of identification with the wider labour movement are more likely to agree with representation, a greater tendency to disagree is shown by those in higher-status occupations, with higher earnings, more favourable perceived prospects for promotion and a higher degree of satisfaction with their status. Those more likely to agree of course show the opposite characteristics. They are also marked out by having spent more time in part-time education, by seeing themselves as having less job security (taking top managers as the reference) and by desiring more. Taken together these variables allow for 72 per cent of total respondents to be allocated to their correct group – with gamma = 0.74 for the association between actual and predicted membership.

INVOLVEMENT IN REPRESENTATIVE BODIES

An immediate problem in looking at involvement in representative bodies is one of definition; how does one decide which kinds of association, or types of representation that may not require a formal association, are relevant? Our solution to this was to try to cast our net very widely and to leave the final decision to the individual respondent. Our method of measuring enterprise unionateness, based on the individual's ordering of a set of statements relating to various levels of militancy, allowed respondents to choose, for example, a body simply 'to consult with and advise employers' (see Appendix). Except for those who agreed only with the statement that they needed no kind of representation, we next asked respondents whether they knew of any type of representative body – trade union, staff association or committee, professional institution and so on – that would be appropriate for the activity(s) that they had agreed with. Thus, where they approved of more than one activity we were not merely asking about the most favoured form, but about organisations falling anywhere within the approved range. We regarded knowledge of the existence of what was seen as an appropriate body as being the minimum degree of positive involvement in a particular body.

Corresponding to variations in the levels of militancy desired by individuals are variations in the character of associations, the extent to which their activities embody greater or lesser unionateness. Although we asked about associations in the context of enterprise unionateness, their characters have also to be considered in terms of society unionateness, the extent of their identification with the wider labour movement.

Whilst in principle there could be a wide variety of associations providing different forms of representation, in practice the great majority of respondents name one of two types, which we shall refer to as trade unions and staff associations. The names suggest that the basic distinction is between externally and internally based bodies, but in fact the various elements of character are so highly inter-related that several other differences are equally clear-cut.

An exception is enterprise unionateness, which does not differentiate the two types so clearly. Partly this is because representation by a staff association can be anywhere on a continuum from a purely advisory form through consultation to full-scale negotiations, though none of the bodies in our sample were at this upper extreme. In addition, although their national character is clear, the extent to which at a local level unions might be prepared to take industrial action is not always as easy to determine. Nevertheless there is a division, in so far as trade unions are clearly committed to negotiation on behalf of their members backed up, if necessary, by the use of sanctions.

Society unionateness distinguishes the two types very clearly. The trade unions were all registered as such (this was prior to the legislation which led to the TUC instructing members to de-register) and at least affiliated to the TUC, if not to the Labour Party; neither was true for any of the staff associations. Thus, on the one hand there are staff associations, lower on both society and enterprise unionateness, internally based and with close ties to a particular employer, and on the other trade unions, higher on both elements of unionateness, externally based and basically independent of any employer. It is worth noting that this pattern is one of the features of private industry not applicable to the public sector, which necessitated separate analysis for the latter.

Some respondents named bodies which we classify as non-unionate, that is not regarding even the mildest form of protection in the field of employment as an important activity. Presumably this indicates the respondent's desire for an existing body to extend its activities into this area. Others favoured bodies lower on unionateness than staff associations, that is engaging in activities relating to employment protection which rarely involved them in direct contacts with employers.

Knowledge of an appropriate body

In Table 2.3 we show the number of respondents in each occupational group who name each of the various kinds of body as most appropriate. Overall, 35 per cent cannot name a body which they consider appropriate, and just as they were previously seen to be less likely to agree with any form of representation, so now we find that professionals

TABLE 2.3 *Respondents agreeing with representation who know of an appropriate body, by type of body and occupation*

Occupational group	None	Non-unionate body	Low unionate body	Staff association	Trade union	Total
Security	8	0	1	0	5	14
Supervisors	58	0	2	17	145	222
Clerks	147	1	0	65	220	433
Draughtsmen	17	1	0	2	49	69
Technicians	94	1	0	12	165	272
Professionals	71	7	8	11	58	155
Managers	58	13	4	12	41	128
Total	453	23	15	119	683	1293

and managers are the groups least likely to know of a body (gamma = 0.38). If we exclude those who named a non-unionate body, on the grounds that its activities are not in fact appropriate, the pattern is essentially unchanged.

We can consider the determinants of knowledge of, or ability to name, an appropriate body in much the same way as we did agreement with representation, that is by carrying out a discriminant analysis. However, whereas previously there were only two groups, now there are five. To avoid unnecessary complication, it seems desirable to reduce the number of groups to three by incorporating the two smallest groups, whose numbers are relatively small, into the group of those who know of no appropriate body. This seems quite reasonable for those who name a non-unionate body, but there is a little more doubt for those naming a low unionate body. However, the latter could not properly be incorporated with the staff associations, since they are all externally based and have little or no contact with a particular employer, as well as being extremely low on unionateness.

Presentation of the results of a discriminant analysis is a little more complicated when there are more than two groups. One discriminant function will distinguish the groups as well as possible, but it is likely that an additional one (or more, up to one less than the number of groups) can add significantly to the discriminating process. This means here that the cases are located in two dimensions, according to their scores on the two discriminant functions. In order to see how each variable contributes to membership in the different groups it is necessary to have a summary indication of the location of the latter in the two-dimensional space. This is given by the group centroids, which represent a 'balance point' of all the members of a group, analogous to the mean. Thus each group is located by its two co-ordinates, and these can be compared with the 'direction' of the contribution of each variable, as given by the values of its coefficients on each dimension. The simplest starting point is to consider just the signs; where the signs of a pair of coefficients are the same as those of a centroid, then that variable can be seen as contributing to membership of that group (and to non-membership if the signs on each dimension are opposite). However, a more adequate view necessitates taking account of the relative magnitudes of both the co-ordinates and the coefficients, especially bearing in mind that the discriminant function on the first dimension contributes more to the differentiation. The reader might find it clearer to sketch a diagram of the kind presented later as Figure 2.1. Again we are able to give an indication of how well actual group membership can be predicted. In this case, of course, the assumption of equal probability reduces the expected frequency of correct allocation to 33 per cent.

In Table 2.4 we have again first considered background factors alone, then introduced in succession social location, expectations and satisfactions, and finally outcomes. As this is done, so the proportion of each group whose membership is correctly predicted increases, as does that of the total. For the most part succeeding factors make for additional information, rather than being simply substitutes for earlier ones. The only exceptions are satisfaction with security, which becomes non-significant when the two unionateness items are introduced, and perceived company status, which is replaced by our own measure of the individual's occupational status.

The greatest improvement in correct prediction overall occurs when enterprise and, more especially, society unionateness are introduced. The latter is clearly the most important single item, as can be seen from its mean value for each of the three groups; those choosing a union have a mean score of 17, compared with 13 and 14 for those who choose a staff association and those who cannot name an appropriate body respectively (the range is from 5 to 25). The differences here are more significant than in any other case. The corresponding scores on enterprise unionateness are 33, 27 and 24 (with a range from 0 to 66). While militancy in relation to the employer does to an extent divide the two kinds of associations, it is less important than the political element of society unionateness. Identification with the wider political aims of the labour movement is strongly associated with wanting the kind of representation that a trade union provides. The fact that those who believe a staff association to be more appropriate are higher on enterprise, but lower on society unionateness than those unable to name any kind of body suggests that an important feature is their deliberate isolation from the wider labour movement.

A further consequence of including unionateness can be seen in the changes in the group centroids. In the first three pairs of columns the tendency is for the first dimension to separate those who name either type of association from the remainder, and for the second to separate those who choose a staff association. In the final pair this latter tendency becomes more marked, but the first dimension now distinguishes those choosing a trade union as most appropriate. The greatest increase in correct predictions also occurs for this last group and in fact, although not shown in the table, there is a much less obvious tendency to underestimate the number falling into it. Previously the numbers choosing a staff association had been considerably overestimated.

TABLE 2.4 Knowledge of appropriate representative associations (union, staff association, low unionate or none) amongst those who agree with representation: discriminant analysis

	Background factors only		Including social location		Including expectations and satisfactions		Including outcomes	
	1	2	1	2	1	2	1	2
Variables: discriminant function coefficients								
Years at school	0.35	0.99	0.36	0.49	0.36	0.44	-0.04	0.47
Part-time (evening) FE	–		0.23	-0.09	0.22	-0.11	0.17	0.15
First job in firm status	-0.81	0.07	-0.67	0.20	-0.64	0.27	-0.32	-0.39
Years of service	0.48	0.18	0.40	0.01	0.39	-0.02	0.08	0.36
Present job status			–		–		0.12	-0.31
Company status			-0.28	0.05	-0.30	0.03	–	
Top manager's income (company)			0.39	0.47	0.39	0.41	-0.11	0.51
Manual worker's income (company)			0.09	-0.52	0.08	-0.50	0.17	-0.09
Satisfaction with security					0.19	0.20	–	
Society unionateness							0.71	-0.35
Enterprise unionateness							0.27	0.28
Relative contribution of functions: per cent	76	24	67	33	67	33	71	29
Group centroids: co-ordinates								
No appropriate body	-0.36	0.04	-0.40	0.11	-0.39	0.13	-0.49	-0.26
Staff association	0.36	0.44	0.57	0.57	0.62	0.56	-0.57	0.89
Trade union	0.18	-0.11	0.16	-0.18	0.15	-0.19	0.43	0.01
Correctly predicted: per cent								
No appropriate body	51		53		53		57	
Staff association	48		58		58		60	
Trade union	46		49		50		63	
Total	48		52		52		60	

Several other factors are worth noting in the last pair of columns. The influence of the status of the first job in the firm is interesting, in that it acts in almost exactly the opposite direction from that of enterprise unionateness and, after society unionateness, is the factor that most distinguishes the three groups. Those unable to name a body started in higher-status jobs (score 133) than those choosing either a staff association (100) or a trade union (98). (Occupation scores are based on the Cambridge Scale (Stewart *et al.*, 1980), adjusted so that the lowest value is zero.) There are significant differences also in the means of the present jobs (153, 124 and 132), but the contribution of this factor is less significant. As can be seen, the trade union group has moved further since starting with the firm, and indeed even more so from their first job. Their first job mean of 89 compares with 101 for the staff association group, which can thus be seen to be likely to have moved down if anything, though they have scarcely moved between their first jobs and the first in the firm. Too much should not be made of this, however, since in large part it reflects the fact that for most of these respondents the two jobs are the same. The majority of those naming a staff association are employed in the two insurance company head offices, which tend to recruit their employees direct from school. As the table shows, naming a staff association tends to be associated with having spent longer at school beyond the minimum age. In contrast, pursuing part-time evening further education serves to differentiate those who choose a trade union.

Another feature distinguishing those naming a staff association also reflects the nature of these two insurance establishments. This is the higher figure that they give, on average, for the income of a top manager. Top management within this industry may well actually earn more than those elsewhere, but certainly since these are head offices they include a level of management which was often above that in the manufacturing establishments that we covered. Nevertheless it is worth noting that these respondents' views of the situation in the wider society seem to be coloured by their local experience, since a similar pattern is found with perceptions of the incomes of top managers in the community (though these do not contribute to the discrimination).

Several of the points relating to the difference between those able to name a union as against a staff association can be checked by an analysis directly comparing these two groups alone. Discrimination between them is quite successful, with 78 per cent of the former group being correctly allocated and 72 per cent of the latter (77 per cent overall). Again society unionateness is by far the best predictor, followed by present occupational status, and the perceived income of an average top manager. Enterprise unionateness, it may be noted, does not make a significant contribution.

We have been concerned so far with a very elementary level of involvement, the ability to name some sort of staff association or trade union that is thought appropriate. It is therefore quite remarkable that the groups are so clearly distinguished. Where organisations are not available within the enterprise this is likely to increase the number unable to name a body, but it appears not to have had much effect. However, availability is probably more relevant to membership since it is easier to name than to join an appropriate body that does not recruit in the firm.

Membership of a representative body

In extending our analysis to consider a higher level of involvement, we shall look at the characteristics not of all members, but only of committed members, that is those who say that they intend to remain in their particular organisation. In terms of numbers this makes little difference, excluding only about 2 per cent of all members, but it does seem to be a more satisfactory indicator of commitment.

Membership of the various kinds of bodies, among those who know of one that is appropriate, is shown in Table 2.5. The proportion of non-members, 42 per cent, is relatively high and it is the professionals and managers who are much less likely to be committed members. It is also worth noting that the proportion of members is higher among those who name a staff association as most appropriate (75 per cent) than it is

TABLE 2.5 *Respondents knowing of an appropriate body who are committed members, by type of body and occupation*

Occupational group	Non-members	Non-unionate body	Low unionate body	Staff association	Trade union	Total
Security	1	0	0	0	5	6
Supervisors	65	0	2	15	82	164
Clerks	106	0	0	48	132	286
Draughtsmen	12	0	0	2	38	52
Technicians	76	1	0	9	92	178
Professionals	49	5	0	8	22	84
Managers	40	11	1	7	11	70
Total	349	17	3	89	382	840

among those choosing a trade union (56 per cent). Knowledge of a staff association implies it is available in the company; this is not necessarily so for a union, and where it is not, joining requires greater effort.

In looking at the determinants of membership of the different groups we can again use discriminant analysis. As before those who are members of non-unionate and low unionate bodies are included with non-members (Table 2.6). When we compare these results with those of the earlier analysis of knowledge of an appropriate body we find a number of similarities. However it is noteworthy that at this level prediction is less successful, particularly for those who are not members of either kind of association, where the results are little better than chance. One reason for this is that the size of this group is consistently underestimated. That is, the individual characteristics which are associated with membership must also be found to a fairly substantial extent amongst non-members. This suggests the importance of availability, a point to which we shall return in a later chapter.

As in the previous analyses the major improvement in prediction occurs with the introduction of the outcomes, of which society unionateness is by far the most important. The mean score for staff association members is again lower than that not only of union members (13 as against 18) but also of non-members (14). The same, this time, is also true of enterprise unionateness (28 as against 36, and 29). Both serve to distinguish union members particularly from non-members in the case of enterprise unionateness and, even more clearly, from staff association members in the case of society unionateness. The important factors for distinguishing this last group are years at school beyond the minimum and perceptions of the earnings of a top manager.

Membership of either kind of body is associated with having started in a lower-status job in the firm. Trade unionists began at the lowest level on average (86), and while staff association members began higher (90), the tendency noted in our earlier analysis for them to have, if anything, moved down (from a first job mean of 103) into their first job in the firm now shows up more clearly. (The union members moved up, on average, from a mean score of 82.)

One point which did not emerge previously is the role of income. The fact that those who earn more are less likely to be members of any representative body is perhaps not surprising, but what is interesting is that when expectations and, later, outcomes are introduced the individual's actual earnings are replaced by what he thinks people like him ought to earn and, in addition, by satisfaction with income. That is, the non-members are the least satisfied and have highest expectations,

TABLE 2.6 *Membership of a union, a staff association or neither, amongst those who know of an appropriate body: discriminant analysis*

	Background factors only		Including social location		Including expectations and satisfactions		Including outcomes	
	1	2	1	2	1	2	1	2
Variables: discriminant function coefficients								
Years at school	-0.65	0.88	-0.39	0.52	-0.38	0.43	-0.13	0.54
First job in firm status	-0.54	-0.95	-0.11	-0.95	-0.09	-0.87	-0.05	-0.83
Income			-0.28	-0.21	–	–	–	–
Top manager's income			-0.59	0.10	-0.55	0.04	-0.40	0.20
Manual worker's income			0.36	-0.28	0.32	-0.21		
Ought own level income					-0.27	-0.29		
Satisfaction with security					-0.26	0.29	-0.10	-0.25
Attitude to management							-0.18	0.03
Society unionateness							0.68	-0.31
Enterprise unionateness							0.22	0.54
Relative contribution of functions: per cent	64	36	77	23	76	24	89	11
Group centroids: co-ordinates								
Member of neither	-0.17	-0.14	-0.16	-0.19	-0.14	-0.21	-0.32	-0.20
Staff association	-0.30	0.39	-0.66	0.35	-0.72	0.35	-0.92	0.45
Trade union	0.23	0.03	0.30	0.09	0.30	0.11	0.51	0.08
Correctly predicted: per cent								
Member of neither	33		31		31		36	
Staff association	52		58		61		61	
Trade union	54		61		64		73	
Total	45		48		49		56	

with the three groups differing more on expected than actual incomes. On average the non-members expect an increase of 23 per cent, as against 22 per cent and 20 per cent for staff association members and trade unionists respectively. Whether these results are to be understood in terms of lower expectations on the part of members, or as reflecting the success of collective representation in securing them higher earnings relative to expectations is clearly an important issue. As we shall see later, the latter is the more likely.

Comparing groups two at a time, in separate analyses, confirms that it is easier to distinguish members of unions from members of staff associations than it is to distinguish members from non-members even among those who know of each type of body. Amongst all members 84 per cent can be correctly classified, with society unionateness again as the major variable by which to do it. Taking just those who know of a staff association, membership can be correctly predicted in 80 per cent of the cases, although the differences in the means of the two groups for most variables considered are relatively small. However one interesting point is that although the actual earnings of members are lower than those of non-members, the average figure they give for what they believe ought to be the earnings of people like themselves is higher.

It is among those who know of a union that membership is most difficult to predict, though even here 69 per cent of the cases can be correctly classified. Once again, society unionateness is the most efficient predictor, together with enterprise unionateness, the perceived earnings of an average top manager and the level of earnings thought right for someone at the individual's own level. In the case of the last two it is the union members who give the lower figures.

All of these comparisons may be combined in one single discriminant analysis using five groups – those who do not know of an appropriate body, those who only know of and those who are members of a trade union, and those who only know of and those who are members of a staff association. Although there are five groups, two discriminant functions account for 96 per cent of the explanation (the first alone accounting for 77 per cent). Thus the groups can to a substantial extent be represented in a two-dimensional space. This time we shall present the results in diagrammatic rather than tabular form. Figure 2.1 shows the most important discriminating variables and the locations of the five groups. The horizontal axis represents the first discriminant function and the vertical the second. Otherwise no particular meaning is attributed to the dimensions. The group centroids are located by their co-ordinates, while the variables are represented as vectors, the direction and magnitude of

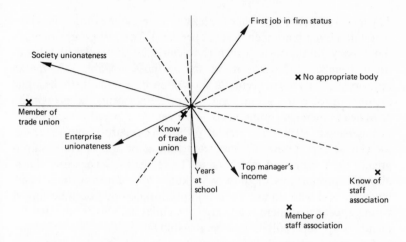

FIGURE 2.1   *Location of five representation groups (centroids) in relation to the major discriminating variables (first two functions)*

which are given by the two discriminant function coefficients. The positive vectors are shown with solid lines, but they may be envisaged as having an opposite, negative counterpart extending 'back' from the origin, shown by dotted lines. The longer a vector, and the more it is directed towards, or away from, a particular group centroid, the greater is its contribution to distinguishing that group. The figure is drawn in such a way as to represent the greater discriminating power of the first function, but its purpose is purely heuristic and too much significance should not be attached to the precise details of layout.

There can be little doubt of the importance of society unionateness, which is the major element in the first discriminant function. This variable clearly divides union members from those who know of or are members of a staff association. In the middle are those who know of, but are not members of a union. Lower enterprise unionateness most obviously distinguishes those unable to name an appropriate body. They are also marked by higher occupational status, in their present job, their first job and their first job in the firm. While the differences in all three are highly significant, the greatest is in the last of the three, and this is the one which enters as a discriminating variable.

Overall, there are a considerable number of errors in classification, with only 44 per cent correct, though this is more than twice as many as we would expect without any information. However, the greatest success is in predicting union and staff association membership (69 and

52 per cent respectively), while the least is in predicting those who know of a union but are not members (12 per cent). This last group are much more likely, on the basis of their characteristics, to be classed either as union members (33 per cent) or among those not able to name an appropriate body (24 per cent). What is interesting is that with the initial assumption of equal group sizes, i.e. of 20 per cent, the proportion classified as members of unions is 36 per cent, compared with an actual membership of 30 per cent. Similarly, though less surprisingly in view of the chance expectation, the predicted staff association membership is greater than the actual membership (15 as against 7 per cent). Since, also, the proportions of those who know of a union without being members and who do not name an appropriate body both decline, it would appear that there is a fairly substantial unrealised potential for membership, especially union membership.

The results are more dramatic when the actual size of each group is allowed for in the classification process. The total proportion correctly classified then increases, to 52 per cent, but there is an overwhelming tendency for cases to be classified either as not naming an appropriate body (51 per cent) or as being a union member (40 per cent). Over one-half of those who know of or are members of a staff association are placed in the former category, as are just under one-half of those who know of, but are not members of a trade union. Most of the remainder are classified as members.

Thus it would appear that the levels of involvement lying between not knowing of any body that would be appropriate for the kind of representation desired (which, judging from the mean enterprise unionateness scores of the individuals in this category, would be of a fairly mild form) and committed membership of a representative organisation are somewhat unstable, in the sense that individuals at these intermediate levels are not clearly distinguishable in terms of their personal characteristics. Rather they tend to be more akin to those in one or other of the groups on each side. As we pointed out earlier, there are comparatively few non-members amongst those who name a staff association as appropriate, so that most of those that we are talking about are respondents who name a trade union.

INVOLVEMENT AS A CONTINUUM

In order to provide a summary of many of the results of this chapter so far, we shall now consider involvement as a continuous variable rather than as three cutting-points. In the interview, those who were able to name an appropriate body were asked a series of further questions designed to assess more precisely the degree of their involvement in that body. Combining our earlier information with these answers we constructed an ordinal-level scale with the following ten scale positions:

(0) No representation
(1) Agrees with representation
(2) Knows of an appropriate body
(3) Has been a member
(4) Is currently a member
(5) Not a member, but is seriously considering joining
(6) Intends to remain a member
(7) Has held office at some time or has attended one or two meetings in the past year
(8) Has attended three or more meetings in the past year
(9) Currently holds office

Some of the scale positions will be seen to form a logical progression, so that the higher position also entails the lower, but this is not always the case. Thus (9) currently holding office entails (4) being a member and (2) knowing of a body, but not (3) having been a member. At first sight the combination may seem confusing, but it simply means that each individual is placed at the highest applicable description. For example (4) currently a member applies only to those few who do not intend to remain in membership, and was introduced to take account of time-lag and inertia among those members whose attachment is really non-existent. Intending to join is included for similar reasons in the opposite direction, and is therefore placed higher in the scale.

Since it is a measure of involvement in representative bodies generally the scale is not really useful until we adapt it by making use of the information that we have on the character of the particular body in which the individual is involved. This is straightforward for those who could name a body as appropriate, in so far as we can treat their score as a measure of involvement in that kind of body. Thus we have several scales, one each for the various types of association shown earlier in Table 2.3. Two problems arise, however: the first involving those who do not name an appropriate body or who disagree with representation, and the second being the question of how those who name one type of body should be scored in relation to other types.

The first problem is relatively easy to solve, since non-agreement with representation and not knowing of a body considered to be appropriate were taken to constitute the two lowest levels of the involvement scale. These two levels can therefore be considered as common to all the scales. The second problem is a little more complicated. We anticipated that, for example, a member of a staff association might also consider a trade union as appropriate, albeit perhaps not to the same extent, and respondents who named one body were always asked whether there was any other which was appropriate. In the event very few named a second body, even in establishments where it was clear that there was at least one alternative available. Whether this indicates simply apathy or aversion to other associations is unfortunately not clear. The latter perhaps should have been checked, though weighing it against disagreement with representation would have created difficulties. If we disregard that possibility there are two solutions. One is to leave out of account all those respondents who name, say, a trade union when considering involvement in staff associations, and similarly for all other types of association. This has the merit of simplicity, but the disadvantage that we are ignoring many of those who agree with representation and thus might be considered to have at least that level of involvement in any kind of body. Thus the second solution is, for each involvement scale, to score those who name any other type of body to the second level (agreement with representation). The problem when that is done is that those at this level may now be a very heterogeneous group, ranging, if we are considering, say, staff associations, from highly committed union members to those who find all available bodies too militant for their taste.

An illustration of this problem is given within Table 2.7. The full table is included to give an indication of the validity of the involvement scale, which may be thought to have been constructed in a somewhat *a priori* manner. It shows the means of enterprise and society unionateness for each level of involvement in associations of different character. Because of small numbers, some categories have been combined overall and others in particular instances. The illustration, which will also serve as an introduction to the general appraisal, is in the two rows of figures associated with scale position (1), those who agree with representation. The upper figure (a) is that for those who, while agreeing, cannot name an appropriate body. This is necessarily the same for each of the distinct types of association. The lower figure (b) differs in each case because it includes all those who name any other kind. In the case of involvement in trade unions, there is little difference between the two figures. We see that for enterprise unionateness this results from a balance between the

TABLE 2.7 Means of society and enterprise unionateness (with numbers in parentheses) by level of involvement in various types of representative body

Level of involvement		Society unionateness				Enterprise unionateness			
		Non-unionate	Low unionate	Staff association	Trade union	Non-unionate	Low unionate	Staff association	Trade union
0 No representation	(a)	12.3 (268)					0 (267)		
1 Agrees representation	(b)	13.8 (453)					25.1 (444)		
2 Knows of appropriate body		15.3 (1270)	15.3 (1278)	15.5 (1174)	13.7 (610)	29.8 (1258)	29.7 (1266)	29.9 (1163)	25.1 (600)
3 Has been a member		13.4 (23)	13.1 (15)	12.4 (30)	15.3 (189)	19.6 (23)	19.1 (15)	23.1 (30)	29.4 (188)
4,5 Considering leaving or joining					16.0 (50) / 16.2 (62)				31.7 (50) / 33.3 (62)
6 Intends to remain member				13.5 (51)	16.8 (141)			29.4 (50)	33.4 (141)
7 Has held office or attended up to 2 meetings				12.8 (38)	17.7 (145)			26.8 (38)	36.3 (144)
8,9 Holds office or has attended 3 or more meetings					18.9 (96)				38.9 (96)
N					1561				1548

higher scores of those involved in a staff association and the lower ones of those involved in low or non-unionate bodies. That is, the latter are less unionate than those who agree with representation but do not know of an appropriate body, while the former, or at least the committed members, are significantly more so. Both groups, however, are lower on society unionateness and this is reflected in the lower alternative score for trade union involvement. Conversely, the higher society and enterprise unionateness of those naming a union raises the alternative scores for each of the other kinds of body.

There is a very clear progression in society and enterprise unionateness as the level of involvement in trade unions rises, with members differing significantly from non-members and, among the former, the active from the passive. Those involved in the milder types of association are, as we have said, generally less unionate than those who simply agree with representation. Only in the case of staff associations and enterprise unionateness is this not true. Even here there is a suggestion that the active members are less militant than other members, though the difference in means is not significant.

In large part the relations between the means of the two aspects of unionateness and involvement in bodies of different character are as anticipated. That is, for associations of a given character, in terms of society and enterprise unionateness, those whose desired levels of unionateness are closest to that character will be the most highly involved. Those whose personal unionateness is lower or, if applicable, higher will tend to be less involved. For trade union involvement the relationship is linear, because these bodies are highly unionate; but for involvement in the less unionate bodies, of which the staff associations are numerically the most important, the relations are more complex, such that, for example, as personal unionateness increases so involvement will at first increase and then decrease. Such complexities, unfortunately, will tend to exacerbate the problem with which we began this discussion and which has still not been resolved. Our original decision was in fact to compromise and to consider involvement in each kind of representative body both with and without those who name some other kind. However the results tended to be so similar in each case that presentation of both was unnecessary. Instead, those using the whole of the sample will be given. In order to make some distinction within the 'agree with representation' category we decided to introduce a new scale position between 0 and 1 made up of those who were involved only in non-unionate bodies.

Tables 2.8 and 2.9 give these results, for trade unions and staff

TABLE 2.8 Influences on trade union involvement (path coefficients)

(a) Background factors only

Father non-manual	Type of school	Qualifications	First job status	Residual
−0.07	−0.11	−0.09	−0.12	0.96

(b) Including rewards and perceptions

Age	Father in trade union	Type of school	Part-time (evening) FE	First job in firm status	Company status	Income	Manual worker's income	Promotion perceptions	Residual
0.10	0.08	−0.07	0.07	−0.15	−0.07	−0.13	0.08	−0.05	0.94

(c) Including expectations and satisfactions

Age	Father in trade union	Type of school	Part-time (evening) FE	First job in firm status	Company status	Manual worker's income	Promotion perceptions	Ought own level earnings	Residual
0.10	0.08	−0.08	0.06	−0.16	−0.07	0.07	−0.06	−0.12	0.94

(d) Including outcomes

Age	Part-time (evening) FE	First job in firm status	Manual worker's income	Top manager's income	Ought own level earnings	Desired status	Enterprise unionateness (linear)	(squared)	Society unionateness (linear)	(squared)	Residual
0.08	0.07	−0.10	0.05	−0.08	−0.09	0.05	0.36	−0.07	0.31	0.04	0.77

TABLE 2.9 *Influences on staff association involvement (path coefficients)*

(a) Background factors only

Years at school	Full-time further education	Residual
0.09	0.11	0.99

(b) Including rewards and perceptions

Years at school	Part-time (evening) FE	Years of service	Present job status	Company status	Top manager's income	Security: manual worker	Residual
0.10	0.06	0.09	−0.15	−0.06	0.12	0.09	0.97

(c) Including expectations and satisfactions

Years at school	Part-time (evening) FE	Years of service	Present job status	Top manager's income	Security: manual worker	Desired status	Residual
0.10	0.06	0.09	−0.15	0.12	0.09	−0.07	0.97

(d) Including outcomes

Years at school	Years of service	Present job status (squared)	Present job status (linear)	Top manager's income	Satisfaction with security	Enterprise unionateness (linear)	Enterprise unionateness (squared)	Society unionateness	Residual
0.11	0.08	−0.05	−0.10	0.11	0.06	0.32	−0.21	−0.19	0.91

associations respectively. Here, since involvement is measured on a scale, we have used sets of path analyses, with the same sort of progressive pattern employed before. In both tables the analysis begins with background factors, and is extended to include social location, expectations and satisfactions, and outcomes. As may be seen, the main increase in explanation comes with the introduction of the unionateness items, which tend to reduce the other factors to non-significance, but the earlier analyses are interesting in pointing to the kinds of persons who are most involved in the two kinds of association.

Trade union involvement is greater amongst those whose fathers were manual workers, and lower amongst those who started in higher-status jobs, went to a selective type of school or who possess a higher level of qualifications. Involvement in a staff association is greater for those who stayed on longer at school beyond the minimum, and lower for those who spent more time in full-time further education.

When rewards and perceptions are included there are a few similarities between involvement in the two kinds of body. In particular those who see their status in the company as lower and those who have had more part-time evening education are likely to be more involved in either. Otherwise, the importance of different aspects of occupational status comes out clearly in the two analyses. In the case of staff associations, in addition to perceptions, there is a similar influence, but rather stronger, from the actual status of the individual's present job. However with trade unions it is the status of the first job in the firm, rather than present status, which is more significant. The statuses of the individual's various jobs are, we know, well correlated, and it is interesting that it is these two which should emerge as the more important in the two cases. As was noted earlier, those who consider a trade union as appropriate have a higher mean current status than those naming a staff association, although on average their first jobs and the first in their present firms were lower. The present results suggests that neither the upward movement in the one case, nor the relative immobility in the other, are directly related to involvement. Rather, it is the present situation which tends to determine the involvement of those concerned with staff associations, and the earlier, more general experience which affects that of the trade union group. This suggests greater concern on the part of the former with their immediate situation, as against a wider outlook on the part of the trade unionists. However, to set against this is the fact that current income is also an influence in their case.

It is worth noting some other influences that are different in the two cases. Trade union involvement is greater amongst older respondents and, even allowing for this, those with less favourable perceptions of their opportunities for promotion. For involvement in a staff associ-ation, perceptions of the earnings of top managers in the company are one of the most important, though as we pointed out earlier in relation to knowledge of an appropriate body this is mainly a reflection of the characteristics of the establishments in which staff associations are usually found.

Little is changed when expectations and satisfactions are introduced. The actual status in society of present job remains the main influence on staff association membership, but desired status replaces that perceived. For the trade union group actual income is replaced by that which the individual believes that people like himself ought to be earning. This again mirrors earlier findings.

Enterprise and society unionateness are by far the most important determinants of involvement, as we have already seen. However their introduction only weakens slightly some of the more important earlier influences. Thus starting in a lower-status job in the firm, being older and having lower expectations regarding income still contribute posi-tively to union involvement. Similarly, lower present job status, longer service, more years beyond the minimum at school and higher perceptions of top management incomes influence involvement in a staff association.

At the beginning of this section we raised the question of possible non-linearities in the relation of the two unionateness variables to involve-ment. In particular there was the problem of the effect of different association characters, where involvement might decrease as individual unionateness increased above the unionateness of the association. Since the hypothetical non-linear relations entail only one reversal of sign they may be represented by a second-order equation. Therefore one approach is to include squared terms for society and enterprise unionateness in the analysis, and following the logic of working with standardised variables we used those obtained by squaring the variable measured from the mean rather than the raw value (this procedure has no net effect on the unstandardised coefficients). As Table 2.8 shows, both terms are significant in the case of union involvement, but their contribution is relatively small. In the case of involvement in a staff association, only enterprise unionateness is significant, but its contri-bution is large.

We can get a clearer idea of the nature of these non-linear relationships by considering them separately and displaying them in a graph. Figure 2.2, which shows the contributions of society and enterprise unionateness to involvement in both trade unions and staff associations, is derived from regression analyses with only the two aspects of unionateness as independent variables. Thus the influence of the other variable is controlled in each case, and in computing the intercept term for each curve we have set the other variable at its mean value.

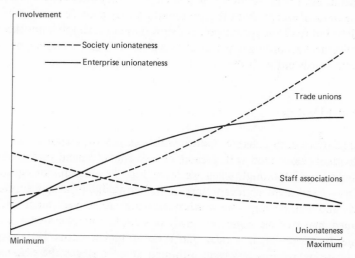

FIGURE 2.2 *Non-linear (second order) contributions of society and enterprise unionateness to involvement in trade unions and staff associations*

For both union and staff association involvement the differences are interesting, and point up some of the arguments that we made earlier. In the case of the former there is a steady increase as enterprise unionateness increases. The slope is steepest at the lowest values, partly because of those respondents who disagreed with representation of any kind and thus received a zero score on both variables. A relatively high level of involvement is reached quickly, and thereafter increasing enterprise unionateness has comparatively little effect. In the case of staff association involvement there is a similar, though less marked, steep start, but maximum involvement is reached at a value of about 40 on enterprise unionateness, roughly corresponding to agreeing most with a representative body to consult with and advise employers. Higher unionateness beyond this point tends to lead to lower involvement.

When we turn to society unionateness there are two differences to note. One is that this aspect of unionateness has a stronger effect on involvement in unions the higher it rises – which is the reverse of the (quadratic) effect found with enterprise unionateness. For involvement in staff associations the curve is of quite different form. It is highest where society unionateness is least, falls quickly, and then evens out as the latter increases. Taken together with the effect of enterprise unionateness we are able to round out further our picture of staff associations. From the enterprise point of view they offer a substitute for trade unions, except that the representation they provide is of a milder variety, but from the society point of view they are a complete antithesis. Involvement according to personal desire with respect to unionateness is wholly consistent with this.

CONCLUSION

The analyses in this chapter indicate fairly clearly the characteristics of individuals associated with greater or lesser involvement in representative bodies. Although when we looked at the three major cutting-points – agreement with representation, knowledge of an appropriate body and membership – we were considering successively smaller sub-groups, many of the same, or closely related, factors operated at each stage. In particular, it is clear that those in higher-status, better-paid occupations are less involved, although at later stages the emphasis shifts to the status of the first job, or the first in the firm, and to higher expectations regarding income.

Other factors tend to be more useful in distinguishing involvement in staff associations and trade unions. The former, especially, tends to be associated with longer service, having spent more years at school beyond the minimum, and having higher perceptions of top managers' earnings. For the latter, it is perceptions of the earnings of manual workers which are more important, suggesting that involvement in trade unions is greater in those establishments where manual workers are better paid.

The results are very similar when involvement is treated as a continuum except that in the case of trade unions there is a stronger indication that older employees and those with a manual or trade union family background are more involved. There is also a more marked tendency for enterprise and society unionateness to improve the explanation. Of course, in looking at each of the cutting-points they were very significant, but usually added only marginally to successful prediction. In the continuous analysis the improvement is considerable; it also shows more clearly, perhaps, the different pattern for the two kinds of representative body, with enterprise unionateness contributing positively to involvement in both, but society unionateness having an opposite influence in the two cases.

3 The Context of Employment

The analysis in the previous chapter (as in our earlier book) has been concerned solely with individual level characteristics. However we were aware that for a fuller understanding, particularly of involvement in representative associations, it would be necessary to be able to set information on individuals within the broader context of the kinds of establishments within which they were employed, the types of representation, if any, available to them, and the behaviour of other workers. Thus, in addition to the interviews with individuals, we collected information from a representative of the management in each establishment and, where there were any, from officials of representative bodies. As we shall describe, we also created some variables relating to aggregates, the establishment or the occupational group, out of the responses of individuals.

EMPLOYING ESTABLISHMENTS

Our general plan in this and subsequent chapters is, first, to consider the question of representation at the level of establishments, then to look at it at the level of occupational groups within establishments, and finally to incorporate the variables at these levels into an individual analysis. Unfortunately the nature of our research design, practically constrained as it was, makes it difficult to consider differences between establishments in a fully satisfactory way. Our decision to select establishments and then to sample individuals within these means that a wide variety of employment situations are completely ignored. Employees in private firms outside manufacturing are represented only by those that we have included from insurance, a few in the construction company and those employed in research laboratories, while those in comparatively small establishments within manufacturing are not represented at all. On the other hand, any other sampling method would have made the collection of data concerning the employing establishment exceptionally difficult, and in any case the kind of employment that we have looked at accounts for a substantial proportion of the total of male non-manual jobs, outside the public sector. Moreover there is still substantial variation in factors such as total number of employees and recent growth rates, as we shall see.

General features of establishments

For each of the 24 establishments in the private sector in our sample we collected information on three major areas: size, growth and bureaucratisation. As far as size is concerned the information that we gathered was in quite detailed form, with the total numbers in the establishment being broken down into males and females and, within each of these, into manual and non-manual and, within the latter, into seven occupational groups. Even ignoring the fine distinctions introduced by this last breakdown, size is not a simple factor. To take the total number of employees alone would mean missing substantial differences in its composition. Our decision was to use the numbers of manual and non-manual workers separately and to consider males only. In the establishments in our sample the numbers of males and females in the two main employment categories are quite highly related, and the reason for taking the numbers of males, rather than the total, was that we thought that this factor was likely to be a little more significant in its influence on the development of collective representation. Again growth, like size, cannot be simply defined, and we chose to use two measures, the increase (or decrease) in the total numbers employed and in the value of sales over the previous five-year period.

The measures of bureaucratisation were taken over from the work of Pugh *et al.* (1968). These were the degrees of specialisation, centralisation and external control of the establishment. The first of these is a measure of the extent to which for each of a set of specific tasks within the organisation there is at least one individual whose responsibility is confined to that task. The second is an indication of the average level in the hierarchy at which a range of decisions is typically made, and the third is derived from this, being the number of such decisions which are taken at a level above the highest in the establishment itself.

Finally, we used one other piece of information. This is the size of the community in which the establishment is located, which may well have an effect on the kind of labour market within which the individual is, and feels himself, involved, and on forms of representation.

For certain of the analyses that follow we grouped the values into categories as follows: male manual employees (cutting-points immediately below 100, 400, 600, 900); male non-manual employees (150, 200, 300, 900); growth in numbers employed (minus 15 per cent, minus 5 per cent, 0 per cent, 40 per cent); growth in sales (0 per cent, 26 per cent, 51 per cent, 101 per cent); size of local community (100 000, 200 000, 500 000). In addition, the measures of the degrees of specialisation, centralisation and external control were reduced to four categories. However, for other purposes, for example looking at the relations among these contextual variables, shown in Table 3.1, we have chosen to dichotomise each variable. The cutting-points were chosen so as to give nearly equal numbers in each category; in those cases where there were four categories as previously described this meant simply combining the first two and the last two, but for the two measures of size and those of growth the split was made within the third of the five categories. Relations are measured by the coefficient gamma. This considers each possible pair of cases to see whether their relative ordering on the first variable is the same (concordant) as their relative ordering on the second variable, or if the ordering is reversed (discordant).

Centralisation and external control are highly related, as can be seen from the table, to some extent necessarily because they are both derived from the same set of indicators. Thus their relations with other variables tend to be rather similar. This is particularly true in the case of the other measure of bureaucratisation, the degree of specialisation. Interestingly, this correlation is negative, contrary to the ideas of the classical tradition – though perhaps too much should not be made of a small sample. Similarly, both are negatively related to growth in sales. However, they are to a greater extent independently related, positively to the size of the community in the case of centralisation and negatively to the number of male manual workers in the case of external control.

The two measures of growth are quite highly correlated, as one might expect. Both tend to be greater where there are more non-manual employees, but size as measured by the number of male manual workers is very strongly associated with a decline in numbers employed.

Collective representation in the establishment

In addition to those features of the establishment, such as its size or its growth in employment, not directly concerned with collective action, there are those concerning arrangements within the enterprise for collective consultation or negotiation, for manual as well as non-manual

TABLE 3.1 Inter-relationships of contextual factors (gamma coefficients)

	Number of male non-manual workers	Growth in employment	Growth in sales	Size of community	Special-isation	External control	Central-isation
Number of male manual workers	0.17	− 0.71	− 0.17	0.32	0.01	0.01	0.17
Number of male non-manual workers		− 0.00	0.60	0.47	0.17	− 0.71	− 0.32
Growth in employment			0.60	− 0.47	− 0.17	− 0.47	− 0.32
Growth in sales				0.17	0.17	− 0.47	− 0.60
Size of community					− 0.32	0.34	0.71
Specialisation						− 0.62	− 0.71
External control							0.96

N = 24

workers. It is in fact useful to begin by considering the position of manual workers in the establishment. This is likely to be of significance for the question of representation of non-manual employees, since it provides a possible model, both positive and negative. That is, as far as the employer is concerned, the development of unionism for manual employees may either pose a potential threat in the form of organisation by non-manual groups, to be countered in various way, or it may lead to an acceptance of representation for such groups. Similarly, for individuals, the existence of manual unions may provide an example to be followed, or one to be avoided as inappropriate or from which distance should be maintained.

The first question, then, is the extent of collective action by manual workers. We asked employers what proportion of the manual workers in the establishment were covered by collective bargaining. In the event, the great majority were either in the nought or 100 per cent category, and the remainder were very clearly divided between those with 'very small' and those with 'very large' proportions. We have therefore treated this as a dichotomy, referring simply to none or all being covered. A related question is the attitude that the employer has towards representation. Here we used the same five statements as in the enterprise unionateness scale, but merely asked which form of representation, if any, was preferred. Because of the small numbers in some of the categories, we decided again to dichotomise the measure. Thus our information is of whether the employer (as far as the representative who completed our questionnaire could judge) favoured a body to negotiate for manual workers which was prepared to take industrial action rather than any milder form of representation.

These two factors are not as strongly related as one might expect (gamma = 0.27). However in this case the marginal distributions are quite markedly different, which makes the results with small numbers less reliable. The more interesting issue in relation to these aspects of representation is the nature of the causal connection between them. It is not clear whether management approval encourages the development of negotiating machinery, or whether experience leads to a (possibly resigned) acceptance. For the present we shall assume that neither has causal priority and defer consideration of the question to a later analysis.

The importance of the different features of the establishment for the determination of collective representation for manual workers is shown in the first two columns of Table 3.2. As before, all variables are treated as dichotomies. Two factors stand out as being of major significance,

TABLE 3.2 *Contextual factors and representation in the establishment (gamma coefficients)*

	Manual workers covered by negotiations	Manual unionateness desired by employer	Salary negotiations	Proportion of non-manual staff in:	
				Trade union	*Staff association*
Number of male manual workers	0.51	0.81	0.68	0.62	0.30
Number of male non-manual workers	0.33	−0.18	0.18	−0.17	0.50
Size of community	0.51	0.30	0.39	0.34	−0.04
Growth in employment	−0.62	−0.18	−0.18	−0.17	−0.50
Growth in sales	0.00	0.50	0.18	−0.17	−0.50
Centralisation	0.00	0.50	−0.18	0.47	0.18
Specialisation	0.87	0.04	0.60	0.32	0.04
External control	0.14	0.39	−0.04	0.32	0.04
Manual workers covered		0.27	0.87	0.46	0.27
Manual unionateness desired by employer			0.51	1.00	−0.14
Salary negotiations				0.81	0.14

N = 24

size as measured by the number of manual workers and the degree of specialisation. In particular, larger establishments have managements which view more militant action on the part of their manual workers with greater favour, while those with greater specialisation are more likely to have a large majority of manual workers actually covered by negotiations. Strangely, however, there is no significant link between specialisation and the employer's attitude. The importance of these two factors is underlined when we extend the analysis. Since we are dealing with only 24 different establishments we cannot make very elaborate breakdowns but we can check on the other relations when the number of manual workers or the degree of specialisation are controlled.

Controlling for the number of male manual workers has an effect of any moment only on the relations involving the other indicator of establishment size, the number of male non-manual workers, and growth in employment. In the case of the former the positive influence on whether manual workers are covered by negotiations is weakened and the negative one on the employer's desired level of unionateness for manual workers becomes stronger. More interesting is the relation between the latter and growth in the number of employees, which reverses sign. Amongst the smaller firms growth is associated, as we might expect, with a lower level of desired unionateness, but of the larger ones all that have grown have managements with a higher level of desired unionateness.

When the degree of specialisation is controlled the relations of several of the other variables to whether or not manual workers are covered by negotiations are dramatically changed. The effect of size as measured by the number of male manual employees is strengthened, but the most notable change involves centralisation. Although this appeared to be unrelated to the proportion of manual workers covered, in fact what we find is that where both specialisation and centralisation are low there are no cases of the majority of manual workers being covered by negotiations, and where both are high there are no cases where they are not covered. There are similar additional interaction effects involving specialisation and both the degree of external control, which is closely related to centralisation, and the size of the local community. Thus, in the latter case, in small communities all establishments with a low degree of specialisation have none or only a few manual workers covered by negotiations, whereas in large communities all those with a high degree of specialisation have all or most covered.

Table 3.2 also provides some information at a general level on the extent of representation for non-manual workers. We asked the management whether any salary negotiations took place in either the establishment or the company. Of these 24 establishments in the private sector, local negotiations took place in twelve, and company negotiations in another three. All but one of the engineering firms had some salary negotiations, which means also that so do most of the large establishments in our sample. One of the two insurance head offices, however, which also came into the largest size category, did not. Thus, as the table shows, the relation with the number of male manual workers is fairly strong and that with the number of non-manual somewhat weaker. The degree of specialisation is again one of the most important of the general characteristics of the establishment.

What emerges most clearly, however, is the value of beginning as we did by looking at the situation as regards manual workers, for it is the fact of whether or not the latter are covered by negotiations which is a major determinant of the existence of negotiations for any of the non-manual groups. In twelve of the fourteen establishments where manual workers take part in collective negotiations there are also negotiations for some non-manual staff, whereas in only three out of ten establishments are there salary negotiations when manual workers do not negotiate. The result is actually more clear-cut, in that one of the three is made up mainly of non-manual employees, while in the other two manual workers are covered by company-wide negotiations.

The effect does not appear to operate through management attitudes. Tolerance of manual worker militancy is associated with acceptance of negotiations for non-manual groups, but the simple relation with desired manual worker unionateness is lower, and disappears when coverage for manual workers is controlled for. There are in fact six establishments where negotiations take place for both manual and some non-manual workers despite the fact that the employer does not approve of a relatively high level of manual worker militancy. Management attitudes concerning manual representation appear to have more influence in establishing negotiations for white-collar than for manual staff, but in both cases the demand from the workers is more important, with manual success having a major impact on non-manual representation.

In spite of its importance, controlling for coverage of manual workers does not greatly affect the relations of other variables to salary negotiations. One interesting point does emerge, though; the two 'deviant' establishments, where there are no negotiations for non-manual workers although most manual workers are covered, are both relatively small in terms of the numbers of the latter, and both also are in the category of employment decline. The example set by manual workers appears to be effective, that is, in those situations where they are of greater numerical significance.

The final two columns of the table are concerned with overall membership of the two major kinds of white-collar representative body, trade unions and staff associations. Information on membership was obtained from local officials of associations wherever possible, but this depended on their being recognised or at least seeking recognition. Where there was not this degree of organisation we had to estimate membership from the responses of our sample. Since we use five broad categories for the proportion in a trade union and three for that in a staff association, our estimates are likely to be sufficiently accurate. In fact for the purposes of the present table we have kept to dichotomies, making the lower category below 20 per cent for trade union membership, and nought for staff association membership.

To a certain extent the higher proportion of employees in a union in those establishments where there are local negotiations than in those where there are not is affected by a division between situations where there are some and situations where there are none, but not entirely so. That there are only two establishments with a fifth of the staff in a union, and none with a third, where negotiations do not take place suggests either that a moderate degree of organisation achieves success or that the lack of recognition inhibits membership. On the other hand there are four instances where salary negotiations take place but there is low membership. In fact one establishment has scarcely any members, though it is exceptional in being a separate research unit within a large company in which negotiations take place.

Other factors which are fairly well related to the proportion who are members of a union are the size of the local community and the three indicators of bureaucratisation. However, there is once again a very clear indication of the importance of manual workers, the number of them in the establishment, whether they are covered by negotiations, and most importantly, the employer's desired level of unionateness for that group. The last appears to have more bearing on union membership among the staff than it has on management's own decisions about recognition. In contrast to the importance of manual workers, the number of male non-manual employees is not significant. Neither are the two measures of growth.

The proportions of non-manual employees in trade unions and staff associations are not significantly related. Greater membership of a staff association is associated with slower growth, both in sales and

TABLE 3.3 *Contextual factors and representation (path coefficients)*

	Number of male manual workers	Number of male non-manual workers	Size of community	Growth in: Sales	Growth in: Employment	Special-isation	Central-isation	External control	Manual workers covered by negot-iations	Manual union-ateness desired by employer	Salary negot-iations	Residual
Manual workers covered by negotiations	0.21	0.26	0.28	–0.04	–	0.69	–0.19	0.49				0.61
Manual unionateness desired by employer	0.49	–0.04	–0.12	0.45	–	0.16	0.50	–				0.73
Salary negotiations	0.29	–	0.20	–0.08	–0.31	–	–0.36	0.22	0.50	0.11		0.74
Proportion of non-manual staff in:												
Trade union	–0.22	0.18	0.05	–0.46	–	0.16	–	–	–0.20	0.83	0.45	0.43
Staff association	–	0.38	–0.42	–0.12	–0.24	0.40	0.78	–0.33	–0.68	0.07	0.20	0.68

employment, and with size as measured by the number of male non-manual employees. Other factors, including the number of manual employees, have little effect, indicating that – in contrast to union membership – staff association membership flourishes where there is a distinctively white-collar concentration of staff.

We can get a clearer idea of the inter-relations among these establishment level variables and the determinants of various aspects of representation by including all of them in a multivariate analysis. In fact, most of the major previous findings are strengthened by the more elaborate path analysis using dichotomous variables shown in Table 3.3. Specialisation is the most important determinant of manual workers being covered by negotiations, followed by external control, rather than centralisation which was suggested earlier. The three measures of size – of the establishment in terms both of manual and non-manual workers, and of the local community – have a roughly comparable influence. The employer's desired level of unionateness for manual workers is most strongly affected, about equally, by the number of male workers, growth in sales and centralisation.

As far as non-manual workers are concerned, we again see that the existence of salary negotiations is mainly dependent upon whether or not manual workers are covered by negotiations, as well as upon the number of manual workers, the size of the local community and where there is external control of the establishment. They are less likely in more centralised establishments and where there has been an expansion of employment. High proportions of non-manual staff in trade unions are to be found most especially where the employer accepts a high level of militancy on the part of manual employees, where salary negotiations take place, and where there has been little growth in sales. On the other hand, there are high proportions in staff associations in those establishments where manual workers are not covered by negotiations, but where there is a high degree of centralisation and specialisation, with a large number of non-manual staff, and where the size of the community is small.

REPRESENTATION FOR OCCUPATIONAL GROUPS

It is now time to refine our analysis of representation at the aggregate level by considering not whole establishments but occupational groups within establishments. In the following chapter we shall be concerned with different occupational groups in terms of the characteristics of their individual members. For the remainder of this one, however, we shall continue with aggregate level analysis. The reason for dealing with occupational groups is that we consider that these are the appropriate minimum units, comparable across establishments, for purposes of representation. In particular, since we wish to examine the effect that availability of a representative body of some kind has in stimulating individual involvement, it is at the level of the occupational group that we have tried to determine whether or not some form of representation is available to an individual in an establishment.

In the case of staff associations the determination of availability is relatively straightforward. Since they are specific to a particular company they can be assumed to be available to anyone who names them, and equally their non-availability is easy to determine. However the situation is more complicated in the case of trade unions, since availability has to mean something rather more definite than simple entitlement to membership. It involves in addition the individual's sense of the suitability of an organisation for people like himself. Since his definition of the latter is likely to include employment in the same establishment, we can consider bodies which are recognised in the establishment or to which other non-manual employees, more particularly those in the same occupation, belong.

So, as a first indication of the availability of an organisation for an individual in a particular job category in a given establishment we have taken the fact of whether there are at least two persons in our sample in that category who are committed members of a particular representative body of some kind. Unfortunately, this criterion alone is not a sufficient measure of the contextual situation. It is possible that a particular group of employees are covered by negotiations even though none of them is a member of any of the bodies which are involved. Strictly speaking, given sampling problems, a reasonably sized minority could be members, without us actually selecting two of them. However we chose to take a membership of two as the criterion, partly to avoid the logical problem where the one committed member was actually the respondent himself, and partly also to avoid giving undue weight to 'aberrant' cases, where for mainly personal or idiosyncratic reasons particular individuals choose to become members of or remain in an association. Similarly we have counted only committed members in order to exclude those whose membership is a temporary carry-over from a previous job.

In addition, as a supplementary criterion, we decided also to regard a particular body as available in those situations where there were a sufficient number of people in the establishment who were members, and where in our judgement that body seemed equally appropriate to some other occupational group. In practice, this criterion was not much used, except that in some cases an internal staff association came to be defined as available for every occupational group, even though none of the members of a particular group may have mentioned it.

We can also consider each representative body in terms of its relation with the employer, that is whether or not it is recognised in the establishment. As previously, we have excluded those associations which do not have employment protection as their most important activity. Thus, applying this distinction and our criteria now gives us four categories relating to availability: no body available; a trade union available, but not recognised; a recognised trade union; and a staff association (necessarily recognised). We should note that these categories also reflect involvement among the workers, and not simply availability to them. However we would argue that this is part of the reality of the situation, since for the individual availability must contain an element of effectiveness, in the sense of support given by those like himself.

A small majority of the total number of respondents in private employment (51 per cent) have a recognised trade union available to them, in the sense that we have defined. Of these, about one-fifth (11 per cent of the total) also have available a staff association. A further 19 per cent have a staff association as the only form of representation recognised by the employer, although for just over a half of these (10 per cent of the total) there is also an unrecognised union available. Five per cent of respondents seem to be in a position to choose all three, but 2 per cent have only an unrecognised union, and 28 per cent nothing available.

It is instructive to look at the situation from the aggregate viewpoint at the level of the establishment. For example, we can present a summary picture of the extent of representation in our sample. In fact it is interesting to try a little more than this, and to examine the question of the extent to which we can discern a process in the development of representation for various occupational groups. That is, are there typically some groups who seek and secure representation before others? Evidence on this is shown in Table 3.4, which has been laid out approximately in the form of a Guttman scalogram, although it is more complicated than a scalogram in so far as an element of intensity is involved (a recognised as against an unrecognised body). Further complications are that not all occupational groups are to be found in every establishment, while in some other cases their numbers are too small to be very reliable; that in five of the cases where there is

TABLE 3.4 *Extent of representation for occupational groups by establishment*

Clerks	Draughtsmen	Technicians	Supervisors	Security	Professionals	Managers
R	R	R	R	R*	R	R
R	R	R	R	–	R*	R
R	–	R	R	–	R	R*
RS	S*	RS	RS	–	S*	RS
US	–	US	–	–	US	US
US	–	US	US	–	US	S
RS	RS*	RS	US	S*	S	S
S	–	S	S*	–	S	S
R	R	R	RS	R	R	0
R	R	R	R	–	R	0
R	R	R	R	–	R	0
R	R*	R	R	–	R	0
R	R	R	R	R	0	0
R	–	0	R	0*	0	0
R	R	R	0	0*	0	0
0	R	R	U⁺	–	0	0
0	0*	0	S	–	0	0
0*	–	0	U⁺	0*	0	0
0	0	0	0	0	0	0
			(seven establishments)			

KEY: R = Recognised trade union; U = Unrecognised trade union; S = Staff association; 0 = No representation; – = No employees in that group; * = 3 persons or less; ⁺ = Craft union.

representation for managers this is because of the presence of a staff association (which, it will be recalled, is used here as a broad term covering any kind of representative machinery, and it is not even always clear whether individuals are involved as staff or management); and that in two cases supervisors have retained membership of their craft union, possibly for reasons quite unconnected with current representation.

Making these various allowances one can see that there is a tendency for clerks, draughtsmen and technicians to become unionised in an establishment before supervisors, and all of these before professionals and managers (security staff are not very numerous, but are in several respects similar to supervisors). Certainly this is the ordering of occupational groups in terms of the proportion of the establishments in which they have some form of representation. A further point which comes out of this table is an apparent strain towards equilibrium, in that very few establishments have unrecognised trade unions for any groups. Thus, either a group secures recognition or support tends to fall away, at least until some new development revives it. The main exception is where an unrecognised union is in competition with a staff association, and such competition can help to sustain interest (cf. Blackburn, 1967). On the other hand, we cannot discount the possibility that in most establishments where recognition was a live issue, a fear of our disturbing the situation led management to refuse us entry.

Following this minor diversion on the extent of availability we can move on to consider its determinants. In doing so we can also consider some other variables which relate to the occupational group. The first of these is the employer's opinion as to the level of unionateness that he considers appropriate for representation of the particular group. This is similar to the variable that we have already used, the employer's desired level of unionateness for manual workers, except that in dichotomising the five unionateness items we have chosen a lower level at which to make the division for the non-manual groups. Secondly, we can refine the two earlier measures of membership among non-manual employees in an establishment, that is to take the proportion of each individual's occupational group within the establishment who are members of, on the one hand, a trade union and, on the other, a staff association. The cutting-points chosen are those nearest the median; for unions this is 20 per cent, but since most groups have no staff association members, the division in this case is between some and none.

Table 3.5 shows the determinants of these six factors. Because all of the variables, including the dependent ones, are dichotomies we again report the standardised path coefficients. Also, as in the previous analysis, we have given equal weight to each establishment – although this does mean that we are not accurately representing occupational groups. One of the clearest results is again the extent to which the existence of a recognised trade union for a particular occupational group depends upon the situation for manual workers. Recognised trade unions are found where the majority of the latter are covered by negotiations and where the employer favours a high level of unionateness for manual workers. Between them these two factors account for one-half of the variance. The first of them, the extent of coverage for manual workers, is also important as a determinant of the employer's desired level of unionateness for the occupational group, leading to a more favourable view, but surprisingly there is only a weak influence from the second. Rather more significant, and all having a positive effect on the employer's attitude, are the size of the community in which the establishment is located, the growth in the number of employees, the degree of external control and the number of male manual workers, while the degree of centralisation has a negative effect.

The degree of coverage of manual workers is important, also, for the

TABLE 3.5 Representation for occupational groups (path coefficients)

	Number of male manual employees	Number of male non-manual employees	Size of community	Growth in sales	Growth in employment	Special-isation	Central-isation	External control	Manual workers covered by negotiations	Manual unionateness desired by employer	Availability of:			Residual
											Unrecog-nised trade union	Recog-nised trade union	Staff associ-ation	
Unrecognised trade union available	—	0.26	-0.13	-0.36	-0.14	-0.18	0.21	-0.54	-0.10	0.20				0.80
Recognised trade union available	0.19	-0.07	0.17	-0.01	0.13	0.16	-0.22	0.20	0.41	0.33				0.67
Trade union available	0.15	—	0.08	-0.22	—	—	—	-0.18	0.29	0.41				0.78
Union recognition where available (weighted N = 843)	0.13	0.10	0.17	0.40	0.01	0.33	-0.19	0.59	0.36	—				0.50
Staff association available	0.15	0.55	-0.10	-0.36	-0.13	0.48	0.19	—	-0.55	-0.21				0.74
Occupation unionateness desired by employer	0.18	-0.02	0.33	-0.16	0.31	0.10	-0.34	0.26	0.40	0.11				0.79
Proportion of occupational group in: Trade union	-0.15	—	-0.09	-0.11	-0.11	0.09	0.05	—	-0.17	0.24	0.36	0.66	—	0.64
Staff association	—	—	-0.13	0.08	-0.03	0.04	0.15	0.02	-0.07	—	0.13	—	0.85	0.37

availability of a staff association, but here it is low coverage that is associated with representation for non-manual workers. It is the number of the latter that has the major positive influence, so that again we have clear evidence of the development of staff associations in situations where large numbers of mainly non-manual groups are employed, and where normal trade unionism has not developed amongst the manual groups. Such establishments also tend to be more bureaucratically organised, at least as regards the degree of specialisation, and to have shown the lowest increase in sales over the previous five years.

Two of these characteristics, of relatively more non-manual workers and low growth in sales, are shown by those establishments where a trade union is available for some occupational groups but is not recognised by the management. Such establishments, however, tend to have lower degrees of specialisation and of external control – that is, they are more likely to be independent units. Surprisingly, although we are dealing with trade unions that are not recognised, their availability is associated with a more favourable view of militancy on the part of the employer, at least as far as manual workers are concerned. As we have noted, though, this does not necessarily mean that non-manual unions are equally accepted.

Another way of looking at the availability of recognised and unrecognised trade unions is to consider, separately, the questions of the availability of a union and the employer's recognition of those that are present in the establishment. As far as availability is concerned, the two most important influences are the same as for a recognised union – that is, representation and the employer's desired level of representation for manual workers. The number of male manual workers and the size of the local community also have positive effects, as they do for a recognised union. The two factors that tend most to inhibit the development of trade unions are external control and growth in sales. These are the ones most strongly associated with the non-availability of an unrecognised union. The reason for this is clear when we realise that these two factors are the ones having the strongest influence on recognition. That is, on the one hand they inhibit unionism, but on the other encourage recognition once a union exists. The other main positive influences are from representation for manual workers and specialisation. This last is interesting in that it illuminates the nature of its indirect influence on involvement in a trade union that we noted earlier. While it has no direct effect on the presence of a union it does lead to employer encouragement through recognition. Also interesting is the one example of a variable which has a strong positive effect on availability but a negative one on recognition. It seems that employers' approval of a high level of unionateness for manual workers results in non-manual unionism which they are reluctant to recognise.

When we turn to proportionate membership in a trade union or a staff association within the occupational group, we can consider the determinants with and without account being taken of availability. Because there is necessarily a strong relationship between availability of and membership in a staff association, when no account is taken of availability the results are very similar to those obtained for availability. For the same reason, when account is taken this becomes the main determinant, and none of the remaining influences are particularly substantial, as shown in Table 3.5.

The position of trade unions is more complicated because of the question of recognition; also, dichotomising membership at the median level reduces the inevitable connection between it and availability, although empirically it does emerge as a strong one. Without taking account of availability (not shown) the major influences are the employer's desired level of unionateness, both for manual workers and for the occupational group. Since the latter in particular is well related to recognition, the pattern for the other variables is more like that for availability of an unrecognised union. The general consequence of introducing the availability factors is to reduce the effect of the other variables, particularly that from the employer's desired level of unionateness for the occupational group. Apart from availability the main influence is from the desired level for manual workers. Aspects of bureaucratisation more or less cease to have any direct bearing, but growth and size factors remain of some significance.

Earlier, we raised the question of the relationship between management's view of militancy and the actual existence of representation for manual workers, and the problem of which could be regarded as causally prior to the other. At that point we left the question open, but it arises again now in relation to each of the non-manual occupational groups. That is, should the availability of a recognised trade union be taken as a determinant of a more favourable view of representation on the part of the employer, or vice versa? Figure 3.1 shows the results of attempting to answer these questions through the use of two-stage least squares analysis. In this model the two variables relating to manual workers, whether few or most are covered by negotiations, and whether the employer regards a high level of unionateness as suitable or not, have been made dependent upon one another, as have the three variables relating to availability and the employer's desired level of unionateness for the individual's own occupational group. It appears from the analysis that availability of a staff association has no influence on any of the other factors, and so for the sake of clarity has been omitted from the diagram.

For technical reasons, and also in the interests of visual simplicity, it was necessary to choose from amongst the basic contextual factors, which are treated as exogenous, only those that make a large independent contribution to the endogenous variables. This results in the structure of effects shown in the figure, where a major point to note is that all of the influences on the availability of a recognised union are mediated through the two aspects of representation for manual workers, whether or not they are covered by negotiations and the employer's desired level of unionateness. There are also influences which, on the face of it, operate through availability of an unrecognised union, but these are better interpreted less as influences on availability as such than on recognition or non-recognition, as may be seen by referring back to Table 3.5.

As far as manual workers are concerned, the results suggest strongly that it is the employer's attitude that affects the situation rather than vice versa. The effect in each direction is only moderate, but that from the situation, the actual coverage of manual workers, to the employer's attitude is in fact negative, the opposite of what might be expected. That is, if anything, experience of having most manual workers covered by negotiations leads management to favour less than the highest level of unionateness. In the case of the nearest equivalent for non-manual workers, the availability of a recognised trade union, the results point less dramatically to a similar conclusion. The effect in each direction is now relatively strong, but that from employer's desire for unionateness to availability is somewhat greater than the opposite one. In fact that tendency is strengthened by an indirect effect. A higher desired level of unionateness tends to lead to the lesser likelihood of there being an unrecognised union available, and of course this in turn is associated with the greater likelihood of there being a recognised union. This reflects employers' preference in the recognition of unions that are already present, while the direct influence is towards the presence of a union which employers want and therefore recognise.

The preceding results on occupational groups have all been for the whole sample within private employment. However, it is easy to see that there are likely to be interaction effects, such that relationships would vary somewhat for the different occupational groups. For example, the development of negotiations for manual workers is more likely to mean

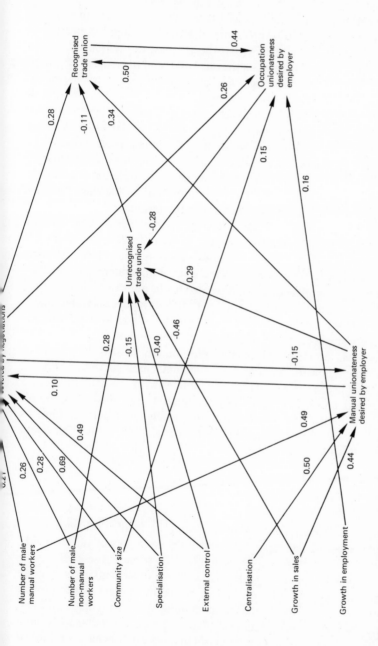

FIGURE 3.1 *Schematic diagram of inter-relationships of representation, employer's attitude and availability of trade unions*

the availability of a trade union for supervisors or clerks than it is for managers. In fact it is not necessary to carry out such a group by group analysis since it is clear, if one looks at availability and the employer's desired level of unionateness, that the sharpest distinction is between professionals and managers on the one hand, and the remaining groups on the other. These two larger groupings are relatively homogeneous and can thus be separately considered.

The presence of interaction effects, at least as between these two major groupings, is clearly shown by the fact that a similar analysis to the foregoing carried out on the sample excluding professionals and managers produces more clear-cut results. Since those excluded constitute only 26 per cent of the total, none of the differences affect the overall nature of the results. However, almost all of the effects become stronger, with a consequent decrease in the residuals.

For only a very few of the managers and professionals is there an unrecognised union available, but the pattern of influences is broadly similar. Availability of a recognised union is much more strongly determined by the employer's desired level of unionateness for manual workers, but the effect of size as indicated by the number of male manual employees reverses direction, such that greater numbers inhibit unionism. There is a similar effect from the number of non-manual workers. External control ceases to influence availability and has a negative effect on the level of membership of a trade union, as also do growth in employment and the number of non-manual employees. As compared with the lower-level occupations the influence of the availability of a recognised union is considerably diminished. For staff associations, both availability and membership, the results are much the same as before. In all cases, the greater homogeneity of the sub-sample again leads to lower residuals.

CONCLUSION

We have presented a considerable amount of detailed evidence in this chapter showing the importance of contextual factors of various kinds. Despite the complexity involved in pursuing some of these relations a general picture does emerge. Probably the major element in that picture is the central importance of the role played by manual workers in the development of trade unionism among non-manual employees. Sometimes this shows up simply in terms of numbers, but usually more significant is the fact of whether or not manual workers have established widespread collective negotiations within the firm and the question of how management views such a development. These are strongly inter-related factors which together demonstrate the extent to which non-manual unionisation depends upon that of manual workers. Management attitudes are not independent of the actual situation in which they develop, but our evidence indicates that approval of unionism, for both manual and non-manual employees, is a significant influence.

Another consistent element in the general picture is probably a somewhat different reflection of the same phenomenon of the importance of the example of manual workers. This is that unionisation is more widespread in larger communities where, we would expect, are to be found larger establishments in general, with more manual workers and thus, on the basis of our results, higher union membership for both manual and non-manual employees. Such a climate seems more likely to carry over into other, small establishments, in a way that it could not in smaller, more isolated communities.

Certain effects of bureaucratisation, as we have measured it, also emerge with relative clarity. External control is another variant of the size and manual worker effect. Thus certain smaller establishments are brought into the system of industrial relations which has been largely shaped elsewhere. As in the case of size of community much of the effect seems to operate through management recognition and the availability of appropriate unions. However the influence of specialisation, which again is particularly important for encouraging recognition of unions by management, is of a different kind. It would appear to reflect a properly bureaucratic mode of organisation which is more consonant, as far as non-manual labour is concerned, with the more systematic treatment involved in collective bargaining. In contrast, centralisation, which is more a reflection of the way in which authority is distributed within the organisation, is generally inimical to unionisation.

To a substantial extent the factors leading to representation through staff associations are simply the reverse of those leading to unionisation. In particular, this development is more likely where the example from and the lead set by manual workers is lacking. However it does also need some positive stimuli, and these are principally size again, obviously in terms of the number of non-manual workers, and specialisation. This last is the major common characteristic of both forms of representation, a fact which strengthens the point made in connection with the development of unionisation. Taken in conjunction with size, and bearing in mind as far as unions are concerned that there is a strong relation between the numbers of manual and non-manual employees, this provides good evidence of the importance of the fit between collective representation and bureaucratic organisation.

4 Availability and its Effects

In this chapter we shall continue the analysis of the availability of representation for different occupational groups, and look at several issues relating to situations that vary according to the pattern and type of available forms of representation. For the most part the analysis will be based on the whole (privately employed) sample, rather than on specific occupational sub-groups. This has the advantage of taking into account a wide range of situations in terms of employment and representation, as well as individual characteristics. While this means that differences between occupational groups may be missed it is worthwhile noting that occupational categories, as commonly defined, do not adequately reflect the structure of different employment experience. In an earlier study (Stewart *et al.*, 1980) we carried out a detailed analysis of clerical workers, including their involvement in representative bodies, of a rather different sort from that pursued here. However, such an analysis would be unduly complex if applied to all of our sample, and would in any case miss certain of the effects that we are able to show. The results of the two kinds of analysis are very much in line with one another, but whereas the earlier book emphasised the stability of experience through career progression, the present one tends to pick out those factors, such as educational experience or first job, which are related to such progression, or perceptions and expectations of promotion directly.

Although we have considered the question of the availability of representation for occupational groups in terms of its determinants at the level of the establishment, this tends to be unsatisfactory in as much as such factors are treated as though they affected all groups equally. As we have seen, however, representation is more likely for some groups than for others. We shall therefore begin this chapter by taking a somewhat different approach and seeing how availability is related to the personal characteristics and employment experience of the individuals making up the occupations. Because our measure of availability is derived from the involvement of individuals within a particular occupational group in an establishment, the results are in many respects similar to those discussed in the second chapter. However, we shall now be talking not about members or those who know of a body, but about all those for whom that body is in our terms available.

We shall again use discriminate analysis, taking three groups: those who have a recognised trade union available to them (whether or not any other representative body is available); those who have a staff association as the only recognised body; and those who have neither. In Table 4.1 are shown the characteristics which discriminate these three groups from one another, and as previously the analysis begins with background factors only, extending by stages to include rewards, expectations and outcomes.

Background factors alone enable a fairly good overall level of prediction, although they tend to classify too many of those for whom no representative body is available into the other two groups. Educational factors constitute most of them, with those for whom a staff association is available being marked out by having spent more years at school beyond the minimum, and fewer in either full- or part-time further education, while the trade union group tend to have lower qualifications. Staff associations are more likely to be available where longer service is the norm. Those with neither kind of body available are most clearly distinguished from the others by the fact that they began their careers in the firm in higher-status jobs.

The most important contribution at the second stage, when social location is included, is from the perceptions of the earnings of an average top manager and an average manual worker in the company, which are associated with the staff association and trade union groups respectively. The former we have discussed previously in relation to knowledge and membership, and the latter too appears to be less a difference in beliefs about the earnings of manual workers than a reflection of different circumstances. There is a much smaller difference between the various groups in their views of the earnings of manual workers generally, and it seems unlikely that groups of respondents in some establishments would exaggerate the figure for those of whom they are likely to have greater knowledge. Rather it seems probable that a union is more likely to be available in plants where manual workers do in fact earn more. As we have shown, union availability for non-manual groups occurs where there is successful unionisation on the part of manual workers. However a question that our research cannot answer is whether their higher earnings are a direct result of unionisation, or

TABLE 4.1   *Availability of representative bodies (trade unions, staff associations or neither): discriminant analysis*

Variables: discriminant function coefficients	Background factors only		Including social location		Including expectations and satisfactions		Including outcomes	
	1	2	1	2	1	2	1	2
Age	—	—	0.34	−0.09	0.33	−0.04	0.35	−0.07
Years at school	0.04	−0.89	−0.38	0.12	−0.35	0.08	−0.32	0.11
Full-time further education	−0.31	0.48	—	—	—	—	0.06	−0.19
Part-time (day) FE	−0.16	0.41	—	—	—	—	0.16	−0.15
First job status	—	—	−0.08	−0.21	−0.06	−0.22	—	—
Qualifications	−0.12	−0.45	—	—	—	—	—	—
First job in firm status	−0.65	0.14	0.04	−0.33	0.04	−0.28	0.01	−0.37
Years of service	0.18	−0.24	−0.31	0.38	−0.30	0.33	−0.25	0.25
Present job status			0.16	−0.22	0.19	−0.17	—	—
Income			−0.16	−0.28	—	—	—	—
Top manager's income			−0.63	0.31	−0.57	0.22	−0.51	0.21
Manual worker's income			0.47	0.39	0.42	0.43	0.42	0.27
Control			0.09	−0.22	0.12	−0.17	0.10	−0.13

	56	44	59	41	60	40	53	47
Security expectations					−0.01	0.14	−0.25	−0.11
Ought own level earnings					−0.26	−0.24	0.10	−0.09
Desired status					0.11	−0.16	—	—
Satisfaction with status					0.04	−0.16	−0.22	0.22
Satisfaction with security					−0.25	0.13	0.11	0.01
Satisfaction with income					—	—	−0.15	−0.25
Attitude to management							−0.09	−0.06
Self-estrangement							0.23	0.16
Society unionateness							−0.11	0.37
Enterprise unionateness								
Relative contribution of functions: per cent	56	44	59	41	60	40	53	47
Group centroids: co-ordinates								
Neither available	−0.48	0.04	−0.02	−0.62	0.02	−0.64	−0.08	−0.74
Staff association available	0.14	−0.55	−0.87	0.27	−0.93	0.23	−0.91	0.39
Trade union available	0.22	0.18	0.34	0.24	0.33	0.26	0.38	0.26
Correctly predicted: per cent								
Neither available	44		53		56		62	
Staff association available	56		60		61		63	
Trade union available	58		65		66		67	
Total	53		60		62		65	

whether both depend upon factors such as the ability of the employer to pay more.

Groups where a union is available, however, tend to have lower earnings, but this is to be expected, given their other characteristics. The interesting question is whether the level of pay is higher or lower than these characteristics would suggest. If it is lower, then it seems unlikely that the employer's ability to pay is the reason for the high manual earnings, while at the same time the question arises why the recognised non-manual unions have not merely failed to raise earnings, but apparently depressed them. The implausibility of this alternative is reinforced by the effect of expectations. Actual income no longer serves to discriminate the groups once expected earnings are introduced because the trade union group tends to have much lower expectations of what people like themselves ought to earn. Unless this is to be attributed to lower expectations as such, it suggests a level of earnings above what would be anticipated.

There are interesting relations of the three job status measures to the classification. All three are positively associated with being in an occupational group with no representation available, but with occupational progression there is a tendency away from contributing to non-availability of a union and towards non-availability of a staff association. This pattern is consistent with the results for individual involvement reported in Chapter 2.

When, finally, outcomes are included in the analysis we find the expected results for the two aspects of unionateness. That is, enterprise unionateness tends to distinguish both of the groups with representation from those without, while society unionateness separates out the union group. This group is also distinguished by a less favourable view of top management. It is interesting also, in view of previous findings, that self-estrangement is linked with non-availability of union representation. This, of course, is allowing for other factors, since the reverse is the case if one simply compares the means. This provides some evidence of the nature of self-estrangement and unionateness as alternative adaptations.

Perceptions of the earnings of other groups continue to have a major influence, in the directions previously described, and several of the variables relating to education remain significant. In particular, the staff association group are differentiated by the fact of having spent longer, on average, at school. They also tend to be somewhat younger, but to have longer service with their present employer. These characteristics are more typical of those employed in insurance.

AVAILABILITY AND MEMBERSHIP

Now that we have a clearer idea of the characteristics of those occupational groups for which the two main types of representative body are available, we can move on to the question of the influence of availability upon membership of an appropriate body. As we saw in the second chapter those individuals whose level of involvement was between non-agreement with any form of representation and committed membership did not constitute a clearly homogeneous group. That is to say, they could not easily be distinguished by their personal characteristics from those placed on either side of them in terms of involvement. One explanation for this may be that there are many people whose individual characteristics are such as would normally make them members of an organisation, but who have none readily available to them.

Before looking at the question of membership, though, we can briefly consider the other major cutting-points on the involvement scale. Most simply this can be done by looking at the differences in the proportions at each point. Thus, for example, where neither kind of body is available only 70 per cent agree with representation, as against 86 and 90 per cent in the other cases. More dramatically, the proportion of those who agree, who also name a union as appropriate, increases from 29 per cent where one is not available to 74 per cent where there is only a union and 52 per cent where there is also a staff association. As we would expect, virtually no one names a staff association as appropriate in those situations where we have not defined one as being available. Where only a staff association is available 24 per cent name it as appropriate, and 28 per cent where there is also a union.

Looking at the same data slightly differently, in terms of cross-tabulations, we find fairly strong relationships between agreement with representation and the availability of either a trade union (gamma = 0.59) or a staff association (gamma = 0.37). However, an even stronger one is found, among those who agree with representation, between the availability of a union and naming a union rather than nothing (i.e. ignoring those who name a staff association) as appropriate (gamma = 0.72). Because there are so few cases of individuals referring to a staff association when one is not available, there is little point in giving comparable figures for that form of representation.

In order to look at the effect of availability of a trade union on membership what we have done is, first, to carry out a discriminant analysis on all those occupational groups for whom there is a recognised union that would be appropriate for them to join. This is the group for whom membership of a union is a relatively easily available option, and we may assume that those choosing not to join do so for positive reasons. Then we have used those variables, appropriately weighted, that discriminate members from non-members in that situation to predict the union membership of those who do not have a recognised union available. Given the fact that the characteristics determining involvement are similar to those that, on average, determine availability, we would of course expect to find fewer members predicted amongst the latter group than are found in the former. However if non-availability is preventing some potential members from joining we should find that this predicted membership is still an over-estimate when compared with the actual.

In fact we carried out two discriminant analyses, including and excluding the two aspects of unionateness. When included they were the best two predictors of union membership and together with the number of years of service in the firm, perceptions of security compared with a manual worker, perceptions of the earnings of top managers and expected or desired earnings, enable the correct prediction of 73 per cent among those with a recognised union available – 68 per cent of non-members and 79 per cent of members. Because it might be thought that unionateness is too closely tied to experience of representation, and to see how successful we could be using more general personal charac-teristics, the analysis was repeated without those two measures. Correct predictions then fall to 58 per cent (53 per cent of non-members and 66 per cent of members), in part because of a considerable over-estimate of total union membership. The discriminating variables are expected or desired income, perceptions of top managers' earnings and of status in the company, and expectations of promotion.

Turning to the second stage, that of the prediction of membership among those without a recognised union available, perhaps the first point to note is that when unionateness is included a potential membership of only 23 per cent is predicted, compared with 31 per cent when it is not. Both figures are considerably higher than the actual union membership of 8 per cent. In fact the discrepancy is even more marked than these figures suggest. Although we are dealing with those for whom there is no available recognised union, some are in situations where there are unrecognised unions. For these, actual membership of 24 per cent compares with predicted membership of 35 per cent using unionateness and 32 per cent excluding it, giving actual to predicted ratios which are close to those of the group for whom there is a recognised union.

However, where no kind of union is available there are only 3 per cent who are members (who must, because of our means of deciding availability be single, isolated members within their occupational group), while 20 per cent or 31 per cent are predicted according to whether unionateness is included or excluded.

Thus two effects are clearly operating. As we have seen there are aggregated individual effects such that where groups of workers share certain characteristics of background, perceptions and so on they are more likely to be organised in a union, but the specifically contextual factor of availability/non-availability has the expected consequence of increasing or decreasing individual membership.

AVAILABILITY AND INVOLVEMENT

The purpose in bringing in information on the availability of different kinds of representative body was that we could then hope to obtain a clearer idea of the relative importance of such contextual influences as compared with those pertaining more to individuals. We can now approach this question in a different way from that in the previous section, by dealing with the whole sample in a path analysis, the results of which are shown in Table 4.2.

This also seems a good point at which to introduce another variable, in a sense an aspect of availability, which is the individual's perceptions of his company management's hostility towards trade union membership. Two items went to make up this, each with five response categories from strongly disagree to strongly agree, with the total score obtained by simple summation of the two. They are:

(1) This company does not really like its staff to join a trade union.
(2) Membership of a trade union would seriously harm my promotion prospects.

Dealing with involvement in a union first we can see, as we would expect, that the availability of a trade union which is recognised by management has a fairly marked influence (it increases values on the involvement scale by about one-and-one-sixth steps on average), much greater than that of an unrecognised union (one-third of a step). There is also evidence that the existence of a staff association, either as a substitute in some situations, or as competition, affects the level of involvement in unions, reducing it by one-half a step. The individual's

TABLE 4.2   *Influence of availability on involvement in trade unions and staff associations (path coefficients)*

	Years at school	Part-time (evening) FE	Years of service	First job in firm status	Satisfaction with income	Enterprise unionateness (linear)	Enterprise unionateness (squared)	Society unionateness (linear)	Society unionateness (squared)	Management hostility to unions	Availability Recognised union	Availability Unrecognised union	Availability Staff association	Residual
Trade unions	–	0.06	–	–0.09	–	0.34	–0.08	0.26	0.06	–0.12	0.21	0.05	–0.09	0.72
Staff associations	0.05	–	0.06	–	0.05	0.32	–0.20	–0.17	–	–	–0.11	0.10	0.28	0.86

view of management's hostility is a further important factor. We cannot directly judge the validity of such views, but they are related to management's approval or disapproval of representation for the occupational group as expressed to us ($E = 0.29$). In any event it certainly appears to be the case that a belief in management's opposition serves to deter people from a higher level of involvement. This is clearly as we would expect in view of previous findings on management attitudes (Blackburn, 1967; Bain, 1970).

The availability of a staff association has a fairly strong influence on involvement in that kind of body, increasing involvement by about one step. The existence of a recognised trade union, as in the reverse case, serves to reduce it (by about one-third of a step), but there is an apparent positive benefit from there being an alternative, unrecognised union. This is probably explained by the fact that in those situations where there is a high level of potential support for some form of representation, there are likely to be some individuals who are members of a trade union, thus making it available on our definition. However, if the union is not recognised, relatively more are for this reason likely to be involved in a staff association. There is reinforcement of this by an effect in the opposite direction, such that where a staff association is strong, recognition is more likely to be withheld from a trade union.

Clearly availability is important, but in view of the element of inevitability (that is availability defined in terms of minimum member-ship within an occupational group) it seems surprising that the effect is not stronger. Clearly, there are a number of establishments where representation is available for many individuals whose involvement is nonetheless of a low order. As our results demonstrate, personal enterprise and society unionateness are still of considerable significance. Few other individual characteristics continue to have a direct effect. However it is still the case that those who began in lower-status jobs in the firm and those with more part-time evening education have higher levels of involvement in trade unions. Equally, longer-service employees and those who have spent more time at school beyond the minimum are more involved in staff associations. In this latter case, too, a previously non-significant effect emerges, that higher involvement is associated with greater satisfaction with income. The main difference when availability is included, however, is that the direct effects from individual characteristics, excluding unionateness, are replaced by those from availability. Since, as we saw earlier, such characteristics are related to availability – and presumably in their contextual effect help to

determine it – the fact that availability adds so little to the explanation is
less surprising.

INVOLVEMENT WHERE REPRESENTATION IS AVAILABLE

There is another way of looking at the effect of availability upon
involvement, and its relationship to individual characteristics, which is
to consider only those situations where people have a serious choice
regarding involvement, particularly at the higher levels. Knowing of an
appropriate staff association where no such body exists in the establishment is obviously problematic, but even though this level of involvement
is possible for trade unions anything higher is clearly very difficult. Thus
it makes sense to consider the more restricted situations where either
type of body is actually available. Since, as we have seen, availability is
related to certain individual characteristics, there will be less variability
in these restricted sub-samples than in the total sample, and hence they
are less likely to contribute so strongly to involvement. Nevertheless it is
interesting to see to what extent they still operate, whether they do so in a
way that is similar to that in the total sample, and whether other factors
become more important.

Looking first at trade union involvement (part (a) of Table 4.3), it is
clear that the differences as compared with the total sample (given in the
previous table – 4.2) are relatively minor. Two individual factors
become significant – both older workers and those with a higher level of
desired status are more involved, while the influence from first job in the
firm becomes non-significant. However, far more important are the
various measures of unionateness and availability, and these show little
change. Perceived management hostility results in lower involvement to
a similar degree, while availability of a staff association has a somewhat
stronger effect. Any change in the relations of the two aspects of
unionateness to involvement is harder to assess because the non-linear
standardised coefficients are more difficult to interpret (especially across
different populations). In this case it is more useful to consider the
unstandardised coefficients (not shown) and what these reveal, in
graphical terms, is that the contribution of enterprise unionateness to
involvement tends to level out more quickly when a trade union is
available. Both this, and the fact that only the linear term for society
unionateness is significant in this case, may almost certainly be
explained by the relatively greater loss of individuals with lower levels of
unionateness, whose level of involvement is necessarily limited. Aside

TABLE 4.3 *Influences on involvement in trade unions or staff associations where the corresponding bodies, or both types, are available (path coefficients)*

(a) Trade union available (N = 976)

	Age	Part-time (evening) FE	Desired status	Enterprise unionateness (linear)	Enterprise unionateness (squared)	Society unionateness	Perceived management hostility to unions	Staff association available	Residual
Involvement in trade union	0.08	0.06	0.08	0.33	−0.10	0.33	−0.13	−0.14	0.76

(b) Staff association available (N = 472)

	Present job status	Enterprise unionateness (linear)	Enterprise unionateness (squared)	Society unionateness	Recognised union available	Residual
Involvement in staff association	−0.11	0.24	−0.21	−0.29	−0.22	0.91

(c) Both available (N = 325)

	Security: manual worker	Ought own level earnings	Intrinsic job expectations	Total satisfaction	Enterprise unionateness (linear)	Enterprise unionateness (squared)	Society unionateness (linear)	Society unionateness (squared)	Residual
Involvement in:									
Trade union	−	−0.13	0.10	−	0.25	−0.13	0.41	0.10	0.86
Staff association	0.11	−	−	0.12	0.31	−0.18	−0.31	−	0.97

from the consequences of this, though, the nature of the relationships to involvement are essentially unchanged.

In the case of involvement in a staff association in those situations where such a body is available (part (b) of Table 4.3) we again find a decline in the contribution of individual characteristics. The only significant effect, which did also show up in some of the earlier analyses, is that those whose present jobs are of higher status tend to be less involved. Availability of a recognised union now has considerably more effect in reducing involvement in a staff association, by more than one whole step. The reason for this is that in the total sample the average level of involvement in such bodies is low, close to the score which is given to individuals who consider a trade union as more appropriate. In the more restricted situation, where the mean level is higher, there is less constraint on being able to reduce the score.

The changes in the contributions of the two aspects of unionateness can also be explained by the differential loss of certain kinds of people in moving to the more restricted group. Individuals with higher levels of enterprise unionateness are more likely to be members of trade unions, and to have a low score on involvement in a staff association. Since there are fewer of these where staff associations are available, the average level of involvement is higher. As can again be shown graphically from the unstandardised coefficients, the effect is for the whole curve to rise more steeply and then to fall off more sharply at the highest levels. Since those high in society unionateness are in any case much less likely to be involved at higher levels in staff associations, there is no similar effect in that case. However there is an effect of availability. That is to say, given that low society unionateness favours higher involvement, this effect will be less marked in the total sample where for many there is no staff association available. Hence, where it is, the negative contribution of society unionateness is a good deal steeper.

Since we have looked at the question of the choice between a trade union or a staff association, in terms of the effect of the availability of one type of body where the other is available, it is worth considering those situations where both types of body are available and in direct competition (part (c) of the table). Once again we find that there is a change in the individual characteristics that emerge as significant. Those more highly involved in trade unions tend to be those with higher intrinsic job expectations, but lower levels of what they believe people like themselves ought to earn; those involved more in staff associations tend to see themselves as having greater security compared to a manual worker and to have a higher level of total satisfaction.

Enterprise unionateness, interestingly, scarcely distinguishes the two groups. In terms of the regression coefficients the two curves are almost identical, with that for staff associations being just slightly steeper at all but the higher levels of unionateness, where both tend to flatten out. In sharp contrast to this similarity, the effect of society unionateness is diametrically opposite in the two cases, as we would by now expect. That is to say, involvement in a staff association declines steadily, while involvement in a trade union increases at a steepening rate with higher society unionateness.

INVOLVEMENT AMONGST THOSE KNOWING OF AN APPROPRIATE BODY

Finally in this chapter we can confine our attention just to those individuals who name a specific body as suitable for the kind of representation they want. There are two reasons for considering this group. One is that this is an extension of the analysis that we have just carried out and will enable us to see whether similar factors operate at this level of involvement as have done so previously. That is, we shall be dealing with those who have, on average, a high degree of involvement, with a majority who are at least committed members – 56 per cent in the case of trade unions and 74 per cent in that of staff associations. A second, more important reason for looking at this group is that it consists of those who see a body as being available, and since individuals name a particular body, we can use information that we have on certain characteristics specific to associations. The data we have at the national level, mainly obtained from a postal survey of all representative associations, are on size and rate of growth over the previous five years, and the industrial and occupational coverage of the organisation. At the local level we know whether the association is recognised for representation, its total membership in the establishment and its membership within each occupational group. These last two have been converted into percentages. In addition, we also asked respondents whether they discussed the affairs of the association they named at least 'fairly often', and whether they thought that in carrying out its activities it was, at least, 'fairly successful'.

To set against actual industrial and occupational coverage we thought it might be useful to ask respondents about the kind of coverage they wanted; specifically, whether they preferred an organisation to cover a single company, one industry or several industries, and to cover just people in their own occupational group, at their own level more widely, all non-manual workers or both manual and non-manual workers. We expected to find that involvement would be higher where the body considered as most appropriate was closest to the individual's desired degree of coverage, but the only clear example of this was for industrial coverage and involvement in a trade union. Even here it appears to be other variables which are more important and some of these relationships are worth drawing attention to. Among the trade unionists, the great majority (87 per cent) are in unions which cover several industries, but only a minority want this level of inclusiveness (26 per cent). Most of the remainder (45 per cent of the total) would prefer a body restricted to their own industry and a substantial number (30 per cent) would like one confined just to their own company. It is those higher on enterprise and society unionateness, who tend also to be of higher occupational status, who are most likely to favour a wider industrial coverage. However their greater inclusiveness does not extend to other occupations. Here, a smaller majority (66 per cent) are in unions which recruit from most non-manual groups and there is a less marked tendency to want a more exclusive body. Those who do, tend to be of higher status and lower in unionateness. However those in unions which are composed largely of manual workers, many of whom are supervisors, are more likely to want a union catering only for those in non-manual jobs, particularly the less unionate among them.

As far as staff associations are concerned, all of course are company-based, but while this is consonant with the wishes of the majority of those who name them as appropriate, there are still 35 per cent who would like a wider-based body. Again, it is those of higher status and who are more unionate who tend to favour wider inclusiveness. Where occupational coverage is concerned, most staff associations cater for all non-manual employees. A few respondents (17 per cent) would like a more general body, but these tend to be low unionate individuals. The more highly unionate would prefer more exclusive representation (30 per cent).

Turning to the general pattern of influences on involvement amongst those naming an appropriate body (Table 4.4), the first point to note is that the explanation using only individual characteristics (part (a)) is less adequate than previously. That is to say, amongst this group, these factors are less efficient in predicting the level of involvement (a similar point has already been made in relation to the discriminant analyses in Chapter 2). Comparing the results with those of the total sample (part (d) of Tables 2.8 and 2.9) we see that several of the same sets of factors operate, but others become non-significant.

Indeed, only two of the variables which were earlier associated with involvement in a staff association remain significant for this more restricted group. These are enterprise unionateness and the number of years of service in the firm. Both of these, however, have an increased effect (i.e. in terms of the unstandardised coefficients), although the reduction in the variance of enterprise unionateness results in a lower standardised coefficient. We no longer find a negative influence from society unionateness, which previously was present because of the large number of those involved in unions who were placed low in the staff association involvement scale. Thus it is clearly the perceived appropriateness of such bodies which is crucially affected, with society unionateness having no significant influence thereafter.

For trade unions, again several of the variables cease to be significant for the more restricted group. Among those that remain the most notable change is the reduced influence of enterprise unionateness. Society unionateness continues to have much the same effect, as also does age. These factors, therefore, operate in a similar manner throughout the involvement scale. The contributions of the perceived earnings of a top manager, and of the expected level of earnings for the individual's own group, however, are stronger.

When certain of the characteristics of the associations themselves are introduced (part (b)) their effects can be seen to be additional to, rather than exclusive of individual characteristics. Only one of the former, however, contributes anything to involvement in a staff association. Those who discuss the affairs of the association at least fairly frequently tend to be more highly involved, although we have to accept here that it is equally likely that being more highly involved leads to more frequent discussion. This same factor operates to much the same extent in the case of trade unions, but a more important element here is whether or not the particular union is recognised in the establishment. Recognition provides an average increase of at least one-and-one-fifth steps in the involvement scale.

Introduction of the factor of recognition is probably the main explanation for the unexpected appearance of a positive term for the square of enterprise unionateness. That is, where there is a recognised union many individuals who are low in unionateness will nevertheless be members. Conversely, without recognition a greater positive motivation is required for the higher levels of involvement.

It also appears that those who name a faster-growing union are likely to be less involved in it. The explanation for this is that there were a substantial number of respondents who were aware of one well-publicised and fast-growing union and who named it as appropriate.

TABLE 4.4   *Influences on involvement in trade unions and staff associations among those knowing of an appropriate body (path coefficients)*

(a) Individual characteristics only

	Age	Years of service	Top manager's income	Ought own level income	Unionateness Enterprise	Unionateness Society	Residual
Trade union	0.08	–	-0.16	-0.14	0.18	0.30	0.89
Staff association	–	0.22	–	–	0.22	–	0.96

(b) Including association characteristics

	Age	Years of service	Top manager's income	Ought own level income	Unionateness Enterprise (linear)	Unionateness (squared)	Society	Growth rate	Recognised in establishment	Affairs discussed	Residual
Trade union	0.10	–	-0.13	-0.11	0.10	0.09	0.27	-0.10	0.25	0.19	0.83
Staff association	–	0.23	–	–	0.24	–	–	–	–	0.31	0.91

(c) Including contextual factors

	Father in union	Years of service	Top manager's income	Unionateness Enterprise	Society	Membership non-manual only	Affairs discussed	Membership in: Occupation	Establishment	Residual
Trade union	-0.07	–	-0.11	0.23	0.13	0.13	0.10	0.42	0.09	0.75
Staff association	–	0.23	–	0.24	–	–	0.31	–	–	0.91

However their involvement was only at this fairly minimal level.

Finally, in part (c), we introduce the two contextual effects, the proportion of membership in the named body both within the establishment and in the individual's occupational group. Neither are significant in the case of staff associations; both, and particularly the latter, are in that of trade unions. Of course there is an element of necessity in the relationship, especially in view of the relatively small numbers in some of the occupational groups in the establishments, but this can hardly be sufficient to explain the quite considerable influence of these factors, in contrast to their lack of influence for the staff associations. The element of necessity applies much less in the case of the proportion of members in the whole establishment than in that of the proportion in the occupational group. However while the correlation with involvement is lower in the former case ($r = 0.43$) than in the latter ($r = 0.55$) it is still higher than that of any of the individual level characteristics, even society unionateness ($r = 0.36$). Thus we are safe to conclude that there is some contextual effect, that is that each individual is influenced in his level of involvement by the behaviour of others, particularly those in the same occupation. However, we should perhaps treat the actual value of the coefficients with caution, since they represent the upper limit of the true effect.

It is also important to note that at this stage there is, to some extent, a replacement of the individual level variables. It may be that with some of these, the two aspects of unionateness for example, the interpretation is that they, too, are influenced by the context, and thus that they previously mediated some of the effects of the latter. However, no such interpretation can apply in the case of age, which ceases to be significant. Thus it is equally likely that the situation is analogous to that noted earlier with respect to availability. It was shown that the availability of a representative body for a particular occupational group in an establishment could be explained to an extent by the characteristics of the individuals making up that group. When availability was itself considered as a determinant of involvement there was some decline in the importance of the individual characteristics. Nonetheless they have to be seen as continuing to exercise an influence, albeit an indirect one. Similarly in the present case those contexts where membership is high are likely to be ones in which a number of individuals possess those characteristics favouring higher involvement, and their effect will in part be mediated through the contextual factor. The latter will in turn, as we have argued, encourage involvement further.

To sum up this chapter, then, there is abundant evidence that

availability of a representative body is an important element in
involvement, which to some extent adds to (or subtracts from)
predispositions derived from purely individual characteristics. As well
as availability in the sense that we have defined it, this also applies to the
fact of recognition (of a trade union) by management, both in the formal
sense and in the less tangible one of respondents' views on their
management's hostility towards trade unions for non-manual staff.

One implication is that in spite of a national trend of membership
growth there are still a substantial number of non-recruited potential
members. Although 'membership types', as defined by the characteristics of members where availability gives a real choice, are mainly
employed in such situations there are nevertheless a good many in firms
where no representative body is available.

The determinants of availability are substantially similar to those
found in an earlier chapter for individual involvement. Even so there is
some tendency for these same factors to continue to apply when account
is taken of availability, but by far the most important individual
characteristics remaining are enterprise and society unionateness.
These, again, tend to be associated with a similar conjunction of factors,
though with rather more emphasis on social background, as was shown
in the previous volume. Thus the general picture is one of representation
being available for those occupational groups in establishments which
are on average less well qualified, of lower status, earning less, who
started in lower-status jobs in the firm and have lower expectations of
their earnings. Trade unionism tends to be associated with the presence
of relatively well-paid manual workers, and the availability of a staff
association with situations where top managers are highly paid.

There is thus a suggestion that representation, especially trade
unionism, is most developed in establishments where non-manual
workers of the kind indicated are more likely to be employed and where
they are most concentrated. We showed in the previous chapter the
kinds of establishments where representation is more likely to be found,
and in that which follows we shall consider the relations between
individual characteristics and general employment situations and the
consequences for involvement.

5 Individual Involvement in Context

In this chapter we shall bring together the aggregate features of establishments and individual characteristics in order to see how far each contributes independently to involvement in collective representation. However, before we deal with the latter, it is interesting to consider the question of the relations between these two units of analysis – that is, whether different establishments tend to employ different kinds of individuals in non-manual occupations. Thus, for example, the social background profile of employees may differ from one establishment to another, and some may offer different levels and mixes of rewards from others. Size might be relevant, in that larger establishments might offer higher salaries or provide better promotion prospects. So also might those that have grown faster, which might also be able to provide greater security. Similarly, the greater bureaucratisation in some establishments might show up in lower intrinsic job rewards. In the first part of this chapter we shall be considering questions of this kind, trying to see whether particular characteristics of establishments are associated with differences in the kinds of people that they employ, and in their reactions to their experience.

ESTABLISHMENT AND INDIVIDUAL CHARACTERISTICS

Although, in this section, we do not report the results in detail our account is based upon the use of analysis of variance techniques. The larger number of categories, as described at the beginning of Chapter 3, have been used for the independent, establishment factors and we have concentrated on describing not simply the significant differences between the means of the independent variables within these categories, but those which show a general tendency to increase or decrease.

In addition to considering each establishment factor singly we also dealt with them as sets. Since they are not independent of one another, this gives an opportunity for identifying spurious relationships or uncovering those that were previously masked. What is done in this case, in effect, is to obtain a set of notional means with control for the effects of the other factors – the values that would be observed if these factors were actually controlled out. This analysis was carried out in each case including the five factors which, allowing for the strength of the relation between them, had the strongest individual relation with the dependent variable. When doing this we also included those individual-level variables that our previous analyses had indicated as significant determinants of the particular dependent variable. No assumptions were made as to which of these influences should be regarded as prior to the others.

Size of establishment and community

As we have demonstrated, some of the most important contextual effects are those involving size, of the establishment or the local community, and we shall therefore begin by looking at these. To relate size to the individual's social background we have chosen to examine four of the major background characteristics; the respondent's age, his father's occupational status, the number of years beyond the minimum that he stayed at school and his level of qualifications. The aspect of size that is in fact most important is the number of male manual workers employed in the establishment. Larger firms, by this criterion, tend to employ in their non-manual jobs older men, from lower-status backgrounds, who have had less schooling and have a lower level of qualifications. When a number of factors differentiating establishments (i.e. including the contextual factors we shall discuss presently) are considered jointly, some of these size effects weaken, but there remain significant differences in age between different-sized establishments, ranging from an average of 37 years in the smaller to 42 years in the larger ones. There is still a tendency, also, for those in the latter to have less schooling and fewer qualifications.

As we move on to social location or rewards, the most important of which are income and status, we find, as we might anticipate from the foregoing, that in those establishments with more manual workers our respondents exhibit lower average occupational status and earnings. However, when the influence of social background and other contextual factors is allowed for, not only do these effects disappear but they reverse direction. That is, those employed in larger establishments can be seen to have reached positions of slightly higher occupational status than would be expected given their age, education and qualifications. Moreover, allowing in addition for this fact, they also tend to be somewhat better paid.

Since many important aspects of perceptions, expectations and satisfactions are determined by individual level factors of the kind that we have already dealt with there is little point in looking at the simple relations alone. Instead we shall concentrate on the results of analyses where a number of influences are allowed to operate together. Then, as far as perceptions are concerned, one point that emerges clearly is that size as indicated by the number of manual workers has a different effect from size as indicated by the number of non-manual employees. So far, indeed, we have commented only on the effects of the former, because those of the latter have been non-significant or considerably smaller. However, in the case of perceptions of the earnings of manual workers and top managers, we find completely opposing influences from the two size variables. Thus in those establishments where there are more manual employees, these workers are seen as being better paid than they are where there are fewer, while top managers are seen as earning less. Where there are more non-manual workers the top managers are thought to earn more and the manual workers less. Assuming that these perceptions are reasonably accurate and that it is not that errors vary with context, it would seem that the less well paid groups of non-manual workers are to be found in those establishments in which such groups also seem to be at an advantage, once account is taken of their background.

The two indicators of establishment size are more in line when perceptions of security and status are considered. Those employed in larger establishments, measured by either criterion, see themselves as less secure and of lower status. In contrast, those employed in establishments located in larger communities tend to see themselves as more secure but, since they also have higher expectations, to be slightly less satisfied.

It is the size of the community rather than of the establishment which is of continuing importance in the determination of outcomes. A lower job attachment of those living in larger communities may well be accounted for by the greater availability of alternative employment, but it is interesting that they also exhibit less favourable attitudes towards top management. Associated with this is a marked tendency to express more unionate sentiments. While it is true for both forms, this is more pronounced in the case of enterprise than society unionateness.

As far as size of establishment is concerned there is little evidence for its effect on any of the outcomes, including unionateness, except that the employment of more non-manual workers does seem to be associated with lower levels of society unionateness. There are significant differences in both types of unionateness between establishments with varying numbers of manual workers, but there appear to be no clear linear trends in these. In fact the greatest differences in adjusted mean values, 18 as against 13 in the case of society unionateness and 45 as against 17 for enterprise unionateness, are between the largest and next-to-largest categories.

To sum up the effects of size, then, it would appear that differences in the number of non-manual workers are of less importance than those in the number of manual employees. Where there are more of the latter are also to be found the older, less formally educated, lower-status non-manual employees who, although they earn less on average, are relatively favoured compared with others of similar personal characteristics. They see themselves, though, as having relatively low status and a lesser degree of security compared to manual workers, whose earnings they see more favourably than do others. However the size of the establishment is less important for outcomes than is that of the community in which it is located. Where this is larger respondents show lower job attachment, a less favourable attitude towards top management and higher society and enterprise unionateness.

Growth

The second set of contextual factors that we consider relate to growth in employment and sales. Again, looking first at the background characteristics of employees, we find a tendency for faster-growing establishments (by either criterion) to employ younger, better-educated people from higher-status backgrounds. When the various contextual effects are considered conjointly the differences are less clear, though that in education remains. Thus, for example, firms that have grown most in terms of sales have non-manual employees who, when allowance is made for other factors, have spent more than twice as long at school beyond the minimum as have employees of the slowest-growing firms (an adjusted average of 1.8 as against 0.8 years).

Again, as we would expect given background characteristics, we find differences in occupational status and income, both of which are higher in the faster-growing firms. Allowing for the effect of background and other contextual factors accentuates the difference, especially where growth is measured by sales. Average annual income, for example ranged from an adjusted average of £1464 in the slowest-growing to one of £2229, in the fastest-growing establishments. Assuming that respondents' perceptions are reasonably correct, manual workers and top managers benefit similarly.

As we would expect, both perceptions and expectations of promotion are higher in those firms that have grown, particularly in terms of sales. However, there is an interesting reversal of relationship between the simple and the conjoint analysis where perceptions of security are concerned. In the former the pattern is again as expected, that those in the faster-growing firms feel more secure, but with the more complex analysis it appears that the sense of security is lower where the numbers employed have grown than where there has been a decline. As we noted earlier, workers feel more secure in smaller establishments, and these are the ones that have grown most. Although we asked about an average manual worker, the comparison is likely to be with those of whom they have the most immediate experience. Thus, since it is likely that in those situations where there have been reductions in the number of employees this has affected manual workers more than the non-manual, the latter are left with a sense of relative advantage. However these linear effects are not the only ones that operate. In each form of analysis it is in the middle category of firms that perceptions are highest. Since this category is one of near-stability, it suggests that change of any kind is unsettling, although the relative impact of growth or decline remains as we have described it.

Satisfaction with almost all aspects of work is higher in the faster-growing establishments, but controlling for the effect of other factors accounts for this. Security is again an exception, in that those in the establishments which have grown most (or declined least) in numbers of employees tend to be less satisfied, although again the highest level of satisfaction is found in the middle category. This presumably reflects the pattern of perceptions.

A similar kind of reversal occurs also with society and enterprise unionateness. Both show some tendency to be greater in establishments where sales have increased least and where employment has declined most rapidly. However it is again the middle category where the level is highest, particularly in the joint analysis which, if anything, suggests that faster decline in numbers employed, far from stimulating greater unionateness, in fact discourages its development. The factor whose introduction brings about this change is the degree of specialisation, which we shall consider shortly.

The individual outcomes are better related to growth in employment than growth in sales, but both forms of analysis point in the same direction. Job attachment is greater where there has been most growth, presumably because of the lesser temptation to move elsewhere, and perceptions of top management are more favourable, even though individual benefits have been allowed for. Conceptions of management's general success, in addition to its personal consequences, seem to be important.

Growth, then, does have beneficial consequences for employees, particularly in terms of income and promotion prospects, although the expectation that it would also be associated with a greater sense of security seems not to be borne out.

Bureaucratisation

Finally there are the three aspects of bureaucratisation to consider as contextual factors: specialisation, centralisation and external control. The first of these show a somewhat similar pattern with respect to social background. That is, establishments exhibiting greater specialisation and centralisation tend to employ people with less schooling and lower qualifications. Even when the affects of other factors are allowed for, employees in the least specialised firms have an average of 2.1 years at school beyond the minimum, compared with 0.8 years for those in the most specialised. Similarly, the adjusted average level of qualifications is higher (3.4) in the least centralised establishments than in the most centralised (1.2).

These differences are related to the kinds of employment to be found in the various establishments, so that the average level of occupational status is lower in both the more centralised and the more specialised firms. In the latter this is accompanied by lower average income, but incomes are actually higher where centralisation is more developed. Thus it is not surprising that when individual factors are controlled for the differences become even more marked, with annual earnings ranging from £1324 in the least to £1764 in the most centralised establishments.

Aspects of bureaucratisation are less important for perceptions than might be expected. Although when each factor is considered separately it does appear that greater centralisation and external control are associated with a lessened sense of security, these relationships become non-significant in the conjoint analysis. We would have anticipated that external control, an indicator of the separation of the plant from those who make final decisions concerning its fate and perhaps also of its vulnerability as part of a large organisation, would lead to greater insecurity. Similarly we would expect that the degree of both specialisation and centralisation would have consequences for intrinsic job rewards, but while there is some evidence for this in the case of use of abilities, the effects are not strong.

Two perceptions do, however, seem to be affected by these factors. Firstly, respondents in more centralised firms tend to see themselves as having lower status, even allowing for their actual occupational status. Secondly, there is evidence that where external control is greater individuals have more favourable perceptions of promotion, although in fact the main distinction is between the highest and second-highest categories.

Centralisation has some other relatively minor effects, in that it is weakly associated both with lower expectations of promotion and lower self-estrangement. More significant is the degree of specialisation, which is strongly related to unionateness. With controls for individual effects, as well as size and growth, the adjusted values of society unionateness increase on average from 13 in those establishments with least specialisation to 17 in those with most, and the differences in enterprise unionateness are of a similar order (19 and 32).

The degree of bureaucratisation, then, at least as represented by specialisation, is an important influence on the development of unionateness, but has little effect on other aspects of perceptions, expectations and so on. However, those employed in the more bureaucratically organised establishments tend to be of lower education and qualifications and employed in lower-status jobs. Allowing for individual characteristics does not remove the contextual effect, but one problem of interpretation is that of whether it is bureaucratisation as such which is having the sole effect or whether there is an additional contextual influence from the fact that individuals of a certain kind are typically employed together. These two effects are most difficult to disentangle, but the latter kind is probably limited in significance. Moreover it may itself be regarded as a consequence of bureaucratisation.

Since specialisation within the establishment was not to any great extent reflected in a decline for the individual in intrinsic job rewards, its importance must be in its more general effects. One which has been emphasised in previous literature is the development of more formal relationships and the decline of administrative particularism (Lockwood, 1958). Our results give support to this view, but to pursue the question further we need to consider in more detail the relation of context to involvement in forms of collective representation. This we are now ready to do.

INDIVIDUAL INVOLVEMENT

The analysis of involvement, in trade unions and staff associations, within establishments can be more detailed. In the first column under each of these two major headings in Table 5.1 are shown the means of involvement in each kind of representative body within the categories of the establishment factors. The second columns give two measures of association for each factor taken singly. That in parentheses (eta) is the square root of the proportion of total variance in the dependent variable explained by the variance of the means of the categories of the factor. The other (R) is a similar measure, but taking account only of linear differences in the means. It assumes equal intervals between the categories and is therefore, given the somewhat arbitrary nature of the category boundaries, fairly stringent.

The clearest linear relationships in the case of both trade unions and staff associations are with size, but with the significant difference that whereas involvement in the former increases with the total number of male manual workers in the establishment, involvement in the latter increases, less strongly, with the number of non-manual workers, and even tends to decrease where there are more manual employees. In fact the highest level of involvement in a staff association is where there are fewest manual workers, and although the overall relationship is non-significant, involvement in a trade union is highest in the next-to-smallest category of non-manual employees. These results are consistent with those that were noted previously – that is that collective represen-tation for manual workers is more likely in larger establishments, and that this in turn influences the trade union situation for non-manual groups. Staff associations, it would seem, develop in circumstances where this influence does not occur, but where size makes itself felt directly.

The only other linear influence of any note upon trade union involvement is specialisation, which we also saw earlier to be a major factor in there being negotiations for both manual and non-manual workers. Involvement in a staff association, however, is negatively affected by both the degree of external control of the establishment and growth in value of sales. It is in fact clear that for both kinds of representation those establishments which come into the highest category of growth are not only very different from the remainder, but even seem to reverse a trend which operates up to that point. That is, there appears to be a general tendency for staff association involvement to increase with higher rates of growth, of either sales or employment, except for the faster-growing establishments, while growth in sales has a similar relation to union involvement.

This analysis can be further extended by considering several of the factors together and seeing what the effect of each of them is when the others are controlled. Because of constraints of the program used (SPSS), we shall consider only the five most important. This analysis takes account of all significant differences between categories, whereas we have so far tried to concentrate only on linear effects. However we can still obtain an indication of the linear influence by examining the means for each category. For trade unions and staff associations the second two columns in Table 5.1 headed 'other factors', show the means and beta coefficients (the multivariate analogue of eta) controlling for the other four factors.

Starting with involvement in trade unions, the first point to notice is the change in the two aspects of size. By itself the number of male manual workers had a relatively strong and clear linear relationship with involvement, but with controls the overall relationship weakens and the linear element seems to disappear. What emerges in its place is a tendency for involvement to decline with greater numbers of male non-manual workers. Involvement is actually highest in the second-smallest category, but the drop between that and the largest category is greater than the difference between any two categories of other factors. The positive relationships are with size of community and, to a lesser extent, growth in sales, but most especially with degree of specialisation. Here there is the next-largest difference of means, and a considerably stronger relationship than when this factor was taken by itself. To some extent it may be the case that unionisation leads to greater specialisation through its effect on personnel management functions. However these constitute only a small part of this measure and it is probable that the more important influence runs from specialisation to unionisation.

While there are important differences between categories in the case of staff associations, none of them are linear in form. The nearest is that with size in terms of the number of male non-manual workers, where this time the greatest difference in means is between the smallest and second-largest categories. There is, in line with the general pattern of findings, a reversal of the situation as compared with unions, since now it is the larger establishments in which involvement is higher.

As well as controlling for other factors it is also possible to introduce the individual characteristics that were earlier found to be related to involvement. If these covariates and the contextual factors are substantially unrelated, then we shall find that considering them together makes

TABLE 5.1 Contextual factors and involvement

	Trade unions						Staff associations					
	Single factors		Adjusted for:				Single factors		Adjusted for:			
			Other factors		Factors and covariates				Other factors		Factors and covariates	
	Mean	R (Eta)	Mean	Beta	Mean	Beta	Mean	R (Eta)	Mean	Beta	Mean	Beta
Number of male manual workers												
less than 100	1.9		3.6		3.3		2.2		1.9		2.0	
400	1.5		2.1		2.2		1.2		1.6		1.6	
600	3.1	0.22	2.3	0.19	2.9	0.12	0.8	−0.13	0.2	0.37	0.4	0.36
900	3.4	(0.28)	3.3		3.0		1.6	(0.27)	1.8		1.8	
900 and over	3.2		2.9		2.7		1.0		1.1		0.9	
Number of male non-manual workers												
less than 150	1.7		3.8		3.2		0.8		0.2		0.4	
200	4.1		5.3		4.0		1.3		1.2		1.3	
300	1.9	−0.01	2.8	0.57	2.6	0.26	0.9	0.16	1.0	0.40	1.0	0.34
900	2.8	(0.25)	3.6		3.0		0.8	(0.27)	2.4		2.2	
900 and over	2.6		0.8		1.9		1.7		1.0		1.0	
Size of community												
less than 100 000	3.0		2.4		2.8		1.3		1.1		1.1	
200 000	1.9		1.7		2.2		1.2		1.2		1.2	
500 000	2.4	0.10	3.2	0.25	2.9	0.11	0.9	0.03	0.7	0.24	1.0	0.15
500 000 and over	3.4	(0.22)	3.3		2.8		1.4	(0.12)	1.7		1.6	
Growth in employment												
less than −15%	2.3						0.9					
−5%	3.2						1.2					
0%	2.6	−0.08	—	—	—	—	1.5	−0.02	—	—	—	—
40%	3.2	(0.25)					1.6	(0.21)				
40% and over	1.1						0.7					

Growth in sales	less than 0 per cent	1.9	0.8	1.7	0.8	0.6	0.5
	26 per cent	2.1	1.9	2.2	1.2	1.8	1.8
	51 per cent	2.9	3.7	2.8	1.7	1.8	1.8
	101 per cent	3.3	2.2	2.8	0.9	0.4	0.4
	101 per cent and over	0.6	2.7	3.2	0.6	0.4	0.5
		0.02 (0.27)	0.32	0.13	−0.12 (0.27)	0.47	0.43
Specialisation	low	1.2	0.5	1.4	1.2	–	–
	medium low	2.7	1.8	1.9	1.5		
	medium high	2.8	2.1	2.8	0.9		
	high	2.9	4.3	3.5	1.2		
		0.15 (0.20)	0.51	0.29	−0.05 (0.12)	–	–
Centralisation	low	2.4	–	–	1.4	–	–
	medium low	2.9			0.9		
	medium high	2.1			1.5		
	high	2.9			1.2		
		0.03 (0.13)	–	–	0.03 (0.19)	–	–
External control	low	2.3	–	–	1.7	1.4	1.4
	medium low	2.9			0.9	1.0	1.2
	medium high	2.6			0.9	1.7	1.5
	high	2.6			1.2	0.9	0.9
		0.03 (0.08)	–	–	−0.12 (0.24)	0.18	0.14
R^2		–	0.23	0.49	–	0.20	0.29

N = 1561. Values less than 0.05 are not significant at the 5% level
– not included in the analysis

little difference. In so far as they are related the effects of the factors, as shown by the adjusted means and beta coefficients, will be changed. Their values when the covariates and factors are taken together, that is with no assumption being made as to causal priority, are shown in the pairs of columns headed 'factors and covariates' in Table 5.1. Since it was necessary to limit the number of covariates, we selected from among the most important, those with the major additional effects, by an analysis which allowed the contextual factors to operate first. One variable which emerged from this process as non-significant for involvement in both trade unions and staff associations, was the perceptions of the earnings of an average top manager in the establishment. The results confirm our earlier suggestion that the importance of this variable is a result of the fact that it reflects the characteristics of particular establishments, in which respondents were correctly reporting on the fact that local top managers were above or below average in earnings.

In the case of staff associations, where individual characteristics were relatively poor at explaining involvement, there is, as we would expect, little change. The variables taken account of – enterprise unionateness (both the linear and the squared terms), society unionateness, years of service in the firm and present job status – add only 9 per cent to the variance explained (as shown by the squared multiple correlations at the foot of the columns) and do not have any marked effect on the means or the beta coefficients. However, bearing in mind that little of the contextual effect is linear, it is less the case that the latter is more important than that neither set of factors is very adequate.

The situation is very different with involvement in trade unions. Here, the individual characteristics that were taken into account – enterprise and society unionateness, the perceived management hostility to unions, age and the status of the first job in the firm – more than double the variance explained. They also tend to reduce the differences in the means between categories and thus to weaken the beta coefficients. However the general nature of the relationships and their relative importance is little affected. Specialisation is clearly the major linear influence, the effect of growth in sales is now essentially linear and there is still a tendency for involvement to decline with greater size as given by the number of non-manual workers.

Thus our results support the arguments that have been made suggesting that bureaucratisation is a significant factor in unionisation. Specialisation, the degree to which administrative roles are subdivided and the parts allocated to particular individuals, appears to be the most important aspect of bureaucratisation. There was no strong evidence earlier that this factor operated through the characteristics of individuals' jobs and we must conclude that the influence is genuinely contextual. Perhaps it is related to technological or other constraints which help determine both degree of specialisation and unionisation.

As for size, which has also often been proposed as an explanation, the interesting point that emerges is the way in which the two indicators of this are differently affected by controlling for other influences. Taken alone it seemed quite clear that it was the number of manual workers which was more important, in a positive direction, but in the joint analysis this is no longer so. Instead it seems that, other things being equal, involvement in trade unions is actually more affected by the number of non-manual employees but if anything is lower the more of these there are in an establishment.

However we must be cautious in interpreting this result. In Chapter 3 we noted the importance of the number of male manual workers in the establishment in determining, directly and indirectly, the proportion of workers in a negotiating body. The indirect affects there were those operating through representation for manual workers. Therefore we now need to consider these factors as well.

We can begin by considering the effects, singly, of the five factors relating to representation. The results of this are shown in Table 5.2. Two of the factors, the proportions in the establishment who are members of a trade union or staff association, are naturally highly related to individual involvement in each of the two kinds of body. They are included mainly for the conjoint analysis, but it is worth noting one or two points here. Where there is a higher proportion of members then obviously some of those who agree with representation are involved at the level of membership in a representative body. However the effect operates throughout the range of involvement, with a higher proportion of office holders and a lower one of those who cannot name an appropriate body. In addition we find that there is also a drop in the proportion who disagree with any form of representation. It is not simply that more of the potential members are recruited, but that the potential membership, in the sense of those in favour of some representative body, also increases. This suggests that individuals may be changed in their basic attitudes towards representation by the fact of its appeal to those around them.

The other factors concerned with representation are better related to involvement in a trade union than in a staff association. The strongest associations are with whether or not there are negotiations for non-manual employees, and with the employer's desired level of unionateness for the representation of manual workers, which we saw was highly related to union membership. The latter suggests that acceptance of unionism on the part of the employer, even more than the actual situation of whether or not most manual workers are covered is a major factor in involvement.

When we consider the factors in conjunction, employer's attitude and the presence of salary negotiations both continue to have a similar level of importance and to make significant independent contributions. As we would expect these contributions are lower when individual characteristics are introduced in the conjoint analysis but remain significant and similar. The effect of whether or not manual workers are covered by negotiations, however, becomes non-significant in both cases.

In contrast this is the only one of the first three factors which has a substantial influence on involvement in a staff association. It is a negative effect which is slightly higher when other factors are taken into account. The presence of salary negotiations also has a small significant effect which is negative when taken singly but changes direction and becomes a little larger with the inclusion of other factors. As before the additional inclusion of covariates makes very little difference.

Table 5.2 also shows the extent to which the pure contextual effects of the proportions who are members of a trade union or a staff association continue to operate, in the former case in spite of its strong association with other factors. When the factors alone are considered these effects increase the relative proportion of variance explained considerably. However, after introduction of the covariates, which again substantially increase the squared multiple correlation, the additional explanation from including the proportions in membership is less, particularly in the case of trade unions.

As a means of summarising the foregoing analyses and of combining all of the variables, we have included them in a regression analysis. This raises a technical problem that we have so far managed to avoid. We kept distinct the two levels of analysis, on the one hand of establishments as units of analysis and on the other of individuals as units. Now we need to combine the two, and since some establishments are larger than others or employ more of those whom we sampled, they are over-represented when individuals are chosen as the units of analysis. Any contextual analysis of the kind that we are attempting comes up against the same problem, that it cannot be 'representative' of both individuals and aggregate units. However, in looking at individual involvement we

TABLE 5.2 *Collective representation and involvement*

		Trade unions						Staff associations					
		Single factors		Adjusted for:				Single factors		Adjusted for:			
				Other factors*		Factors and covariates*				Other factors*		Factors and covariates*	
		Mean	R (Eta)†	Mean	Beta	Mean	Beta	Mean	R (Eta)†	Mean	Beta	Mean	Beta
Manual unionateness	low	1.9	0.30	2.1	0.22	2.4	0.12	1.3	−0.05	1.2	0.00	1.2	0.02
	high	3.6		3.3		3.0		1.1		1.2		1.2	
Manual workers covered by negotiations	none	1.9	0.18	2.8	−0.03	2.5	0.03	1.7	−0.25	1.9	−0.32	1.9	−0.30
	all	2.9		2.6		2.7		0.9		0.9		0.9	
Salary negotiations	no	1.2	0.31	1.5	0.26	2.2	0.09	1.3	−0.06	0.9	0.13	0.9	0.11
	yes	3.1		3.1		2.8		1.1		1.3		1.3	
R^2					0.14		0.45				0.07		0.20
Proportion of non-manual staff in: Trade union	1% or less	1.0	0.46	1.3	0.40	1.9	0.28	1.3	−0.03	0.9	0.10	0.8	0.12
	2% to 19%	1.7	(0.47)	2.0		2.1		0.8	(0.23)	1.1		1.1	
	20% to 29%	2.4		2.3		2.3		1.7		1.4		1.3	
	30% to 49%	3.3		3.1		3.1		1.1		1.2		1.3	
	50% and over	5.0		4.8		4.1		0.9		1.3		1.3	
Staff association	Nil	2.7	−0.07	2.6	0.02	2.7	0.06	0.8	0.39	0.8	0.39	0.9	0.34
	1% to 10%	2.7	(0.09)	2.7		2.7		1.0	(0.44)	1.0		1.0	
	over 10%	2.1		2.6		2.3		2.5		2.4		2.2	
R^2			—		0.23		0.49		—		0.21		0.30

* The first three factors have been adjusted only for one another (i.e. not for the two remaining).
† *Eta* is identical to *R* in the case of dichotomised variables.
$N = 1561$. Values less than 0.05 are not significant at the 5% level.

are in little doubt as to the correctness of analysing individuals and thus accepting the fact of different-sized establishments. Size may be taken as a correct weighting of importance.

The results of the regression analysis are presented in Table 5.3. We have chosen to treat the contextual variables as dichotomies for several reasons – the overall number of establishments, the limited number of categories of the variables and the non-linearity of some of their inter-relationships. The table gives the unstandardised regression coefficients, since for dichotomies these are readily interpretable as changes in the intercept term. However, since the dichotomised variables have very similar standard deviations they can also be directly compared for relative importance.

In considering the results of this table it is useful to refer back to Table 3.3 where we looked at the structure of relations between the establishment variables, in order to understand the structure of indirect effects which lie behind the direct influences shown here. For example, the consequences of including or omitting the pure contextual influences from the proportions who are members of trade unions or staff associations become comprehensible. As we would expect, when they are included they emerge clearly as the most important influences on involvement. However in the case of trade union involvement exclusion of these factors leads to only a very slightly lower proportion of variance explained, so that the explanation is almost as good without them. The most obvious result of excluding them is for the effect from there being salary negotiations to become stronger, and for the formerly indirect influence from the employer's desired level of unionateness to become a direct one. Both of these are positively associated with involvement and all of the remaining influences are negative.

The two major depressing influences are from the number of manual employees and the growth in employment, and both have to be seen in relation to certain of the indirect effects. In particular while it is true that overall union involvement is higher in larger establishments, this is because where there are more manual workers there are more likely to be negotiations for non-manual employees and a more favourable attitude towards unions on the part of the employer. On the other hand, the tendency for there to be a lower level of involvement in establishments that have grown comes out more strongly when indirect effects are taken into account.

The direct effects of the different aspects of bureaucratisation on union involvement are weaker at this stage, and their influences appear to operate mainly indirectly, through the situation created for manual

TABLE 5.3 Contextual factors and involvement (regression coefficients)

	Number of male manual workers	Number of non-manual workers	Size of community	Growth in: Sales	Growth in: Employment	Special-isation	Central-isation	External control	Manual workers covered by negotiations	Manual union-ateness desired by employer	Salary negot-iations	Proportion of non-manual staff in: Trade union	Proportion of non-manual staff in: Staff association	Perceived management hostility to unions	R^2
Perceived management hostility to unions	0.64	−0.45	0.86	0.69	0.55	0.78	–	0.32	–	−1.16	−1.11	–	1.01	–	0.20
Involvement in trade union (a)	−0.52	−0.50	–	0.77	−0.74	−0.02	−0.50	–	–	–	0.91	1.65	–	−0.26	0.21
Involvement in trade union (b)	−0.85	–	–	–	−0.91	–	−0.61	–	−0.53	1.53	1.72	–	–	−0.24	0.20
Involvement in staff association (a)	–	0.22	0.09	–	–	–	–	–	−0.22	−0.22	–	0.34	1.45	–	0.21
Involvement in staff association (b)	−0.21	0.66	−0.25	−0.55	–	0.43	0.88	−0.36	−1.03	0.28	0.24	–	–	–	0.16

(a) = including the contextual effects of proportions in representative organisations.
(b) = excluding the contextual effects of proportions in representative organisations.

workers. However, there is a clear tendency for involvement to be lower in more centralised establishments.

When we turn to involvement in staff associations the picture is rather different. Here, involvement is higher in those establishments which have higher levels of both centralisation and specialisation. Since these effects did not show up in the earlier analyses, it would seem that they are offset by other influences. The results suggest that staff associations and unions are responses to different types of situation, the former developing where non-manual workers are more directly affected by bureaucratic organisation. The two insurance company head offices are the most obvious examples. Further, involvement in such bodies is strongly influenced by size in terms of the number of non-manual workers, again in contrast to involvement in unions, and it is much less likely in establishments where most manual workers are covered by negotiations. Thus it would seem that extensive unionisation of manual workers inhibits the development of staff associations and encourages non-manual unions. However in the absence of such developments among manual workers, perhaps because of their small numbers, size and bureaucratisation lead to the development of consultative and representative machinery.

Introduction of the pure contextual factor of the proportion of workers who are members of a staff association considerably reduces the effect of the other variables. Whereas in the case of involvement in trade unions it was possible to achieve almost as high a value for the squared multiple correlation coefficient without these factors, in this case it is not so. Again we find that explanation of staff associations as a phenomenon is more difficult than is that of trade unions.

Table 5.3 also gives an indication of which establishment factors lead individuals to believe that the management in their company is hostile towards trade unionism. Clearly these beliefs are strongly influenced by management's actions. Most obviously this is shown by the fact that where salary negotiations take place less hostility is thought to exist, but that this is also true where management expressed to us greater tolerance of manual worker militancy indicates that a more general industrial relations climate within the establishment is important.

Apart from these two, only one other establishment characteristic leads to a lower level of perceived hostility, and that is the number of non-manual workers. This particular effect has to be taken in conjunction with that from the proportion of such employees who are members of a staff association. Management encouragement of staff associations obviously tends to be seen as a deliberate anti-union policy. Other than this the major influences leading to greater perceived hostility, allowing of course for other effects, are larger communities, more specialisation, growth and greater size in terms of manual workers. As the table also shows, the beliefs in management hostility to unions are not without effect, since they do tend to reduce involvement in trade unions.

CONTEXTUAL AND INDIVIDUAL INFLUENCES

Having considered in some detail the influences on involvement that derive from the nature of the establishment and the employer we are now in a position to integrate with these the individual level effects that were discussed in earlier chapters. We shall begin by considering the part played by the latter in shaping those factors that relate to the whole occupational group in the establishment, namely the availability of representative bodies and the level of unionateness that the employer considers desirable, and then return to the question of involvement in both trade unions and staff associations.

The technical difficulties in an analysis combining establishment, group and individual level variables are increased when each type features among the independent variables, since the first two types will show considerably less variation between individuals than will the third. Whether or not this also means that they cannot strictly be regarded as independent observations is a matter about which argument is possible. In our view the identical nature of certain experiences for groups of people is a fact that must be taken into account. Certainly it would appear foolish not to consider an analysis of the kind undertaken here. However one result of the different degrees of variability has to be borne in mind. This is that there will necessarily tend to be stronger relationships where establishment or group level variables are involved.

Thus, for example, in looking at the top row of Table 5.4 we find, as we would expect, the major determinants of the employer's desired level of unionateness are those factors relating to the establishment. Approval of representation is more likely where a majority of manual workers are covered by negotiations, in plants located in larger communities and which have grown most in terms of number of employees. It is less likely in establishments with a higher degree of centralisation and where sales have grown most. However there are some individual level effects. One of these varies comparatively little within occupational groups, and we have already suggested it is likely to be important. That is, the higher the status of an occupation, the lower is the level of unionateness that the employer considers appropriate. It is lower, also, the more subordinates that an individual sees in an average working day, a result which almost certainly reflects the fact that managers, who are slightly lower than professionals in terms of status, are the group for whom representation is seen as least appropriate.

In the two cases of the availability of an unrecognised trade union or of a staff association the only individual level variable is the status of an occupational group. Both kinds of body are less likely to be available for higher-status occupations. However, for the existence of a trade union which is recognised we again find that the indicator of hierarchical position, the number of subordinates seen in a normal day, is significant. Interestingly, also, some of the influence of occupational status is taken over by income. That is, on this interpretation it is not simply the lower-status occupations that have a recognised union available, but those that are lower paid. However it would be dangerous to assume simply that it is low pay as such which is important. It is equally plausible that this factor is no more than an indicator of the background of the individuals typically in an occupation in a particular establishment and of the kinds of work that they typically perform.

One other factor affects both employer's unionateness and the availability of a recognised trade union. This is the individual's perception of the earnings of an average manual worker in the same establishment. In so far as these perceptions are accurate, then they represent an indirect measure of what is in fact an establishment level variable. What is indicated is that it is in establishments where manual workers earn more that managements are more likely to have a favourable view of representation and to recognise trade unions for some non-manual groups. Since these also tend to be establishments where a majority of manual workers are covered by negotiations this suggests that the influence from lower pay noted earlier is more likely to reflect the kinds of persons employed than the fact that they are paid less than comparable workers. We cannot wholly discount the possibility that the effect is real, and that indeed it may run from representation to pay. Then the gains of manual workers through negotiations could be seen to lead to the creation of representative machinery for non-manual workers, the effect of which would be actually to worsen their relative position, perhaps through the general effect of negotiation upon relativities. However in the light of previous evidence that apparently low-paid employees in establishments with large numbers of manual workers, who were seen as relatively well paid, were actually at an

TABLE 5.4 *Contextual and individual influences on representation for occupational groups and involvement (path coefficients)*

	Number of male manual workers	Number of male non-manual workers	Size of community	Growth in sales	Growth in employ-ment	Central-isation	Special-isation	External control	Manual workers covered by nego-tiations	Manual union-ateness desired by employer	First job in firm status	Income status	Subor-dinates number	Manual workers income	Occupa-tion union-ateness desired by employer	Perceived manage-ment hostility to unions	Unionateness Enter-prise	Unionateness Society	Residual
Occupation unionateness desired by employer	–	–	0.40	–0.41	0.34	–0.25	–	–	0.43	0.26	–	–0.16	–0.08	0.11					0.70
Unrecognised trade union	–	0.20	–0.19	–0.40	–	0.24	–0.26	–0.65	–	0.30	–	–0.19	–0.08	–					0.75
Recognised trade union	–	–0.06	0.21	–	–	–0.27	–	–	0.34	0.43	–	–0.07	–0.08	0.05					0.64
Staff association	0.07	0.53	–	–0.53	–	0.11	0.46	–	–0.55	–	–	–0.14	–	–					0.65
Trade union involvement	–0.11	–	–	–	–0.11	–0.14	–	–	–	0.20	–0.06	–	–	–	0.15	–0.13	0.33	0.26	0.72
Staff association involvement	–	0.18	–	–0.17	–	–	–	–	–0.24	0.09	–	–0.09	–	–	–	–	0.25	–0.17	0.90

advantage when their background was taken into account, this seems an unlikely possibility.

Since it is measured at the individual rather than the group level, involvement in the two major kinds of representative body is, as we would expect, less strongly related to the contextual factors. The two aspects of unionateness have the strongest effects, with the by now familiar pattern of involvement in either a union or a staff association being determined positively by enterprise unionateness, while society unionateness has opposing effects in the two cases. Other individual effects, however, are relatively weak. Status – of the present job in the case of staff associations, and of the first job in the firm in the case of trade unions – has a small direct effect, in addition to a substantial indirect one through unionateness. The remaining effects are from characteristics of the establishment, although this does include one, the individual's perception of management's hostility to unions, which is indirectly so. Involvement in a trade union is likely to be higher the less the individual thinks that his local management is against trade unions for people like himself, as well as the more that management actually is more favourably disposed towards representation either for his occupational group or for manual workers. Once these factors are allowed for, the tendency is for involvement to be lower in establishments which are more centralised, have grown more in number of employees and are larger in terms of the number of male manual workers employed.

Neither the employer's attitude nor our respondents' beliefs about them are of significance for involvement in a staff association, except that it is slightly greater where there is approval of more militant action on the part of manual workers. However involvement in this kind of body is lower where most manual workers are covered by negotiations. It is lower, also, in establishments that have grown quickly in terms of sales and higher where non-manual workers are employed in greater numbers.

Availability has not yet been considered in this analysis of involvement, because it is interesting to see how good the explanation is without including variables which, as was explained earlier, are necessarily strongly related. In fact it is an indication of our success in this respect that their introduction makes only a very slight difference. In the case of trade union involvement, although this is well correlated with the availability of a recognised union for the occupational group (lower only than with those of the two forms of unionateness), introduction of the latter leaves the residual virtually unchanged. The only effects that are more than slightly altered are those from the three variables relating to the employer's attitude, which all become weaker. Thus, clearly, the three together carry rather more information than the availability indicator. Since they are well correlated with the latter, very little additional contextual influence is provided by availability.

The existence of a staff association is more important for involvement in that kind of body, partly because of the fact that such existence is a necessary condition for even the low level of involvement implied by knowledge of it. Even here, though, the residual is only reduced to 0.87. Again the effects from society and enterprise unionateness are essentially unchanged, but that from the proportion of manual workers covered by negotiations is substantially weaker.

INVOLVEMENT IN RELATION TO OTHER ADAPTATIONS

Having considered involvement as it is influenced by both individual and contextual factors we are now in a position to be able to extend the model presented in the previous volume which showed the relations among the various outcomes or adaptations. This model is based on the use of two-stage least squares regression analysis, in which any variable involved in a reciprocal relation, directly or indirectly, is replaced by its estimated value using the exogenous variables. Our concern has been to try to bring out the general structures of relations, by deleting nonsignificant effects, rather than to derive precise.values for coefficients. However we believe that the latter do give an indication of relative importance.

To the earlier model we can add both the contextual factors as possible determinants and, most importantly, involvement in either a staff association or a trade union. In fact we did also begin by including those contextual factors which might possibly both affect and be affected by involvement, and perhaps also be related to some of the other outcomes, that is availability of the different types of representative body and the level of representation for the group favoured by the employer. However none of these emerged as being involved in any kind of reciprocal relation, although as we have seen they may be significant as simple determinants. Thus, for example, the kind of representation desired by the employer has an influence on union involvement, but there is no effect in the opposite direction. Equally, the analysis confirms the previous indication that when other contextual factors are taken into account availability of a recognised trade union does not influence involvement, and neither is there any support for the idea that the effect might run the other way. (In the case of staff associations availability was not included as a determinant because of the high level of necessary relationship with involvement.)

The model, which includes the two forms of involvement and the individual's perception of management hostility to unionism, is shown in Figure 5.1. The inclusion of these variables and the relations involving them results in only one change to the structure of influences among the other variables taken on their own as in the original model. This is that there is no longer an effect back to promotion expectations from attitude to top management. This new model confirms that the major significance of the latter is to mediate between job attachment and unionateness. Job attachment itself emerges more clearly as central to the loop of influences involving the individual outcomes.

The results in the model for the individual's perception of the degree of management's hostility to unionism confirm our findings that where individuals believe that their company takes an unfavourable view, and that membership of a union might harm their promotion prospects, their level of involvement tends to be lower. It is perhaps worth noting that there is no significant effect, either positive or negative, the other way, but a more interesting new insight from this analysis is the way in which these perceptions of management's opinion serve as a link between self-estrangement and union involvement. Those who believe that their management is hostile to unionism are likely not only to be less involved, but also to exhibit a higher degree of self-estrangement, suggesting that the two outcomes are alternatives. Moreover, the existence of a strong reciprocal effect from self-estrangement indicates a way in which that form of response tends to inhibit union involvement.

The influences upon and between the unionateness items do not change from those in the previous analysis but the new model gives a clearer idea of how they are associated with union involvement. There is a very strong effect from enterprise unionateness, but no direct influence from society unionateness. However greater involvement in a trade union does increase society unionateness directly, but not enterprise unionateness. Thus the major pattern of effects is that higher society unionateness leads to higher enterprise unionateness, which in turn leads to greater involvement in a trade union. Involvement itself serves to increase society unionateness. (This structure of effects at a single time should not be interpreted as a continuous loop of effects over time.) However it is also worth noting how these direct influences in one direction compare with the indirect effects which lead back the other way. Thus the direct effect of enterprise unionateness upon involvement

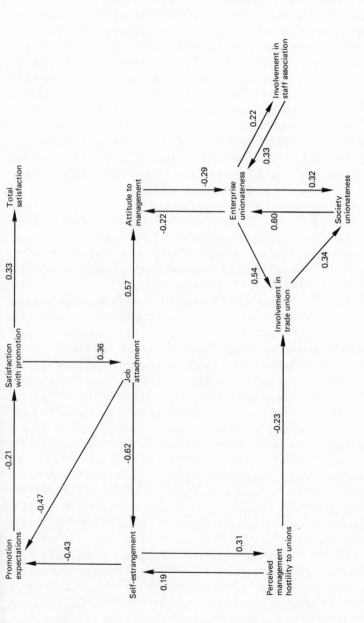

FIGURE 5.1 *Schematic diagram of inter-relationships of outcomes, including involvement.*

is considerably greater than the indirect one (through society unionateness) in the reverse direction, but the influence of the two aspects of unionateness upon one another can now be seen to be much less unequal, and even more, the indirect effect of society unionateness upon involvement is virtually the same as the direct effect the other way. Since society unionateness is largely determined by more general social influences this means that the latter are indirectly having an effect upon involvement. Equally, though, union involvement stimulates identification with the wider labour movement.

The position of involvement in a staff association within the model is straightforward, since it appears to depend only upon enterprise unionateness and in turn to influence only that variable. This perhaps is not entirely surprising in view of our findings that availability and membership are more difficult to explain in the case of staff associations than trade unions. What is of interest, though, is firstly that there is no direct relationship between involvement in the two kinds of body, where one might have expected a negative effect from each to the other, and secondly, that the influence of involvement upon enterprise unionateness is greater than that in the other direction.

The relative isolation in this model of staff association involvement and society unionateness is both instructive and serves as a warning against taking the results too literally. Certainly it makes sense that little is related to involvement in a staff association apart, as we would expect, from enterprise unionateness. However the model implies that attitudes to management and society unionateness have the same indirect effect on involvement in each type of body, except for being less strong in the case of staff associations. This is hardly in line with earlier findings, particularly for society unionateness which has consistently emerged as differentiating the two forms of representation. Bearing in mind the non-linear relations between involvement and the aspects of unionateness it seems in part, that the simplified linear model fails to capture the full pattern, probably because of interaction effects. In fact there is a negative influence from society unionateness to involvement in a staff association which, though non-significant, would outweigh the apparent indirect positive effect.

It is consistent with our argument from earlier results that society unionateness, the more class-conscious aspect of unionateness, should arise mainly from experience in a wider context and influence union involvement through the more 'trade union conscious' enterprise unionateness. (The model also indicates a small, non-significant direct positive effect, as we might expect.) The reverse influence, from involvement to society unionateness, suggests that experience of trade unionism does tend to increase class consciousness.

The final point worth drawing attention to is the way in which the various measures relating to a collective adaptation favouring change are linked to the more individual outcomes of avoidance. In the previous model it was attitudes to top management which provided the link with the unionateness items, and this remains, as we have said. The other link we have described operates on involvement directly, but it also goes through a variable which concerns perceptions of management, that is their hostility towards unionism. We saw in the previous volume that it was the individual adaptations which were best accounted for in terms of our general model of perceptions, expectations and satisfactions, and that they tended to be influenced by a different set of factors from those items concerned with the collective response. In particular, intrinsic job rewards were much more important for the individual outcomes, whereas social location, especially income and occupational – and thus hierarchical – position, was more significant for unionateness and involvement.

It appears that the individual and collective adaptations are responses to different areas of concern to the individual. However there are connecting links between them which, as we have noted, run from the individual to the collective types, but not the other way. Enterprise unionateness, the desire for representation, develops as an alternative to the individual outcomes as a result of top management coming to be blamed for the situation. This tends to be translated into involvement in a representative body, particularly a trade union, although in that case fear of management hostility has a restraining influence – or conversely a belief in management's approval or tolerance serves as encouragement. At the same time we should note that the greatest influence on enterprise unionateness is from society unionateness, identification with the labour movement arising mainly from factors outside the work situation.

UNIONISM IN THE PRIVATE SECTOR

We have considered a number of different types of explanation that may be offered to account for variations in white-collar unionism. Clearly the workers' attitudes are one important element and these may be related to personal characteristics or experience of employment. They are an aspect of current experience in that they must relate to actual circumstances. Thus they entail perceptions and expectations as well as evaluations and feelings of commitment. Many features of the employment situation – such as size, growth and bureaucratisation of firms, reward and career structures – have a wider influence than simply on individual experience; they may also affect availability and employers' attitudes and willingness to negotiate. Also, one feature of the work situation is the type of people employed there, which is related to other features of organisation and technology through recruitment policy and possibly self-selection by workers according to their orientations.

We have approached the possible forms of explanation in a variety of analyses. Each entails some degree of simplification and no one set of results should be accepted uncritically. What is important is not so much the detail of each analysis as the persistent pattern that emerges throughout. We shall return to this in the concluding chapter but it may be useful to note a few salient points here.

Of the various individual characteristics the ones that emerge as especially important are the two measures of unionateness. Enterprise unionateness is related to support for either a staff association or a union while society unionateness, reflecting support for the wider labour movement, is related negatively to involvement in an internally oriented staff association and positively to union involvement. Nevertheless many union members would prefer a more narrowly based organisation.

Other individual characteristics that are important include status in terms of background, past and present jobs, with high levels inhibiting involvement. We saw that professionals and managers are significantly less likely to agree with representation, know of an appropriate body or be committed members. However it is low status early in a career which is more clearly related to union involvement, while present status has more bearing on support for staff associations. Older workers have greater involvement, though in the case of staff associations this is essentially length of service. Education differentiates the organisations in that staff association supporters tend to have spent longer at school while union supporters are more likely to have taken part-time courses. In keeping with low status, low pay is also associated with involvement, although there is some evidence suggesting that those covered by negotiations are relatively better paid when account is taken of their other characteristics, such as levels of qualifications. This brings in the nature of the employing organisation, as does the tendency for union involvement to coincide with a perception of relatively high pay for manual workers in the firm whereas for staff association involvement it is high pay of top managers.

The main contextual influences are size and bureaucratisation, as might be expected from previous research. However the form of their operation is interesting. Staff associations appear to be a response to situations where there are a large number of non-manual staff directly influenced by bureaucratisation, but they are less likely where the employer negotiates with manual unions. On the other hand it seems that the influence of size and bureaucracy on non-manual unions operates indirectly through the manual workforce. One important factor is the influence of this on management's more favourable, or at least tolerant, views about unions. Another appears to be the impact of example and general outlook, which is further supported where the firm is located in a large community. Furthermore the unity of influences must be recognised, in that those men with the relevant backgrounds are also more likely to be employed in contexts favouring union involvement. Probably the single most pervasive theme is contact with manual workers in a variety of ways, from background, earlier career stages and present work situation.

The fact that the availability of a union can be explained by the same set of factors as involvement, and does not operate as an intervening variable, is important. It means that unionism, as represented by its presence and the degree of support, can be explained directly in terms of the situation and experience of the employees. This is clearly relevant to the question of the relation of class and class consciousness to unionism. However the limited coverage of the analysis should be recognised. It has concentrated mainly on background factors, treated largely as personal characteristics, and the current work situation and rewards. While this has entailed location in the wider society in various ways it has not done so completely. Yet a full theoretical account of trade unionism must place it in the context of the whole society, including the nature of 'market' relations and the role of the state.

There are good methodological reasons for the restricted nature of the analysis so far and we believe the results are of considerable interest. However within this sort of approach there is one significant way in which we can extend the empirical analysis to help us draw more general conclusions. This is through an analysis of public sector unionism, to which we turn in the next chapter.

6 Trade Unionism in the Public Sector

Most of this volume is devoted to unionism in the private sector because there is considerably more variability there than in the public sector. As unionisation in the latter is very much higher, there is consequently relatively little individual variation. Equally, there is greater uniformity with respect to terms and conditions of employment, and contextual factors. The most significant of these are highly centralised, so that the effective number of 'employers', whatever the legal situation, is very limited – indeed, at certain times, and perhaps increasingly, tending to just one, the government in conjunction with the Treasury.

We argued in the introduction that public sector employment was of great significance for our understanding of the processes of stratification in industrial society. The public provision of resources entails, at both practical and theoretical levels, a direct breach of understanding of inequality in terms of market processes. In so far as it represents a redistribution of resources to employees in general and to disadvantaged groups in particular it has class connotations. For many public employees there is a double interest in public provision; they are at one and the same time consumers of the resources and employed to provide them. In this chapter we shall examine two related issues, the influences upon individual involvement in trade unions in the public sector and the class character of membership. To some extent we shall do this by providing an internal analysis, as we have done on a much more extended scale for the private sector, but we shall also try to see what major differences and similarities there are between unionism in the two areas of employment.

Table 6.1 shows the variations in involvement in representative organisations by occupational level and sector of employment. Because numbers in the public sector are lower than in the private sector (especially among supervisors and draughtsmen) we have collapsed the occupational distinctions into managers and professionals against the rest. We saw when discussing the private sector that this was, in any case, the most significant dichotomy.

The contrast between the sectors is very marked. In the public sector 75 per cent of all employees are in some sort of organisation concerned with employment as against 31 per cent in the private sector. The figures for membership of full trade unions are 55 per cent and 24 per cent respectively. We have stressed at various points that our respondents are not a random sample of white-collar employees and it is worth noting that the contrast in the general population is probably even more marked. The method of stratifying our sample produced a higher proportion of trade union members in manufacturing industry than other figures (Bain, 1970; Bain and Price, 1972) suggest is present in the wider population.

Turning to the top of Table 6.1, only 3 per cent in the public sector disapprove of representation as against 17 per cent overall in the private sector and 31 per cent among managers and professionals. Of those who approve of representation only 8 per cent in the public sector do not know of an appropriate body for the kind of representation they prefer. Given the wide availability and visibility of organisations in the public sector it is unlikely that even this group are ignorant of any representative body. Rather, their failure to name a body probably represents a strong preference for a representative organisation of a particular kind. In the private sector over one-third of all who agree with representation say they do not know of an appropriate body. It seems safe to assume that this represents in part a much lower level of availability of *any* type of representation rather than merely a preference for a particular, non-available type, though the very high figure for managers and professionals may reflect a particular shortage of organisations with the features of their desired forms.

Something similar may be operating for both the groups in the private sector who know of an appropriate organisation, but are not members. It should be remembered that naming an appropriate organisation does not mean that it is available in their establishment, so some of the difference between sectors is accounted for by differential availability. Nevertheless, even when we consider only those situations in private employment where unionate organisations are available for the different groups, we still find lower levels of membership overall than in public employment (41 as against 72 per cent) and lower levels amongst managers and professionals than among others (23 as against 45 per cent).

In both sectors managers are more likely to be members of non-

TABLE 6.1 Comparison of involvement of managers and professionals with lower-level employees in both public and private employment

	Public			Private		
	Managers and professionals	Others	Total	Managers and professionals	Others	Total
Those who disagree with representation as a percentage of all in the occupational category	5	2	3	31	12	17
Those who know of no appropriate organisation as a percentage of those who agree with representation	5(10)*	10(12)	8(11)	46(63)	32(40)	35(46)
Those who are not members as a percentage of those who know of an appropriate organisation	15(24)	17(26)	16(25)	58(84)	38(63)	42(69)
Members of non-unionate bodies as a percentage of all members	6(28)	2(28)	4(28)	25(86)	0	2(70)
Those in mild representative organisations as a percentage of all members of unionate bodies	31(51)	17(41)	24(45)	33(92)	18(70)	22(76)
Members of full trade unions	49(100)	59(100)	55(100)	8(100)	30(100)	24(100)
N	160	197	357	411	1150	1561

* Figures in parentheses give cumulative percentages of the total.

unionate bodies, although the numbers involved are very small. Most of these people in the public sector are senior local government officials who are members of very specialised small organisations. Although a higher proportion of all members among managers and professionals in the private sector are members of non-unionate bodies, because membership of any body is relatively low, this represents an even smaller proportion of all managers and professionals than in the public sector.

It is when considering membership of mild representational bodies as opposed to full trade unions that we first see a distinction between occupational levels in the public sector. There is a clear break from the pattern we have observed at lower levels of involvement. Whereas in the private sector managers and professionals have had consistently lower levels of knowledge and involvement than clerks, technicians, etc., it has been impossible to separate the occupational groups in public employment until now. However the division of members of unionate bodies between mild organisations and full trade unions is very similar in both sectors and the variations between occupations is also well matched, with managers and professionals almost twice as likely to be in mild organisations. We outlined in our companion volume (and we shall shortly turn to an analysis of this issue here) how enterprise unionateness was much the same for all groups in the public sector, while society unionateness varied by occupation. In Chapter 2 of this book we saw that in the private sector organisations exist which match the pattern of unionateness of higher-status groups. That is to say, staff associations provide for a relatively high level of enterprise unionateness coupled with a low level of society unionateness. In the public sector there are bodies which are similar in the sense of being internal to a single employing organisation, and some even include the term 'staff' in their name. The similarity in fact goes beyond this, because these bodies tend to favour the slightly milder forms of enterprise unionateness and, more particularly, are low on society unionateness. It is this lack of identification with the wider labour movement, marked especially by their non-affiliation to the TUC, which most strongly suggests their closeness to staff associations in the private sector. However, since they are usually classed as trade unions, we shall refer to them as such, but distinguish them from the less problematic bodies by calling them mild trade unions. It is these bodies that are included under mild representative organisations for the public sector in Table 6.1. The private sector organisations are staff associations.

There are more who name as appropriate and are members of 'full' trade unions than mild organisations in both sectors. In public employment this reflects, in large part, the nature of our sample, since the great majority of those naming the mild trade unions are employed in central government, where these are the only kinds of bodies available for all groups except the clerks. Most respondents in local government and the public utility included in our sample name full trade unions. Generally, the likelihood of an individual being a member, given that he sees a body as appropriate, is much the same for both kinds of union – over 80 per cent. Because of the pattern in central government employment there is a tendency for the mild trade unions to be more frequently named by professionals and managers than by the other groups (gamma = 0.30) and for it to be more likely that they will be members if they do name one (gamma = 0.32). The first of these patterns was not seen in the private sector, and it would seem that although the generally greater pressure towards collective representation in public employment draws in the higher-level groups it is partly because they have available to them bodies of less unionate character. The other pattern, of greater willingness to join the milder unions which are named than to join full trade unions which are considered appropriate, is common to both sectors, and in fact is less marked in public employment. Again it is an indication of the kinds of representation that such groups are drawn towards. However we should not lose sight of the fact that even among managers and professionals in the public sector the majority are members of a representative body which undertakes collective bargaining.

In order to consider involvement in more detail we can carry out a discriminant analysis, as we did earlier for the private sector. Because the numbers who disagree with representation or who do not know of an appropriate body are so small, there is little point in performing the analysis using either of those cutting-points. It is more useful to look at members of the two kinds of trade unions against the remainder who agree with some form of representation. The results are shown in Table 6.2, which is again arranged so that the effect of introducing successive sets of factors can be seen. In fact, background alone provides much of the explanation obtained, with just four factors enabling 52 per cent correct prediction of group membership (compared with 33 per cent by chance). Reflecting what we have already seen in terms of the different occupational groups, we find that three aspects of education, the number of years spent at school beyond the minimum and in full-time or part-time further education, are important in predisposing against membership of full trade unions. However it appears also that those with longer service are more prone to favour the mild unions.

TABLE 6.2 *Membership of a trade union, a mild trade union or neither, amongst those who know of an appropriate body in the public sector: discriminant analysis*

	Background factors only		Including social location		Including expectations and satisfactions		Including outcomes	
	1	*2*	*1*	*2*	*1*	*2*	*1*	*2*
Variables: discriminant function coefficients								
Years at school	-0.04	0.38	0.26	0.27	0.12	0.34	–	–
Full-time further education	-0.44	0.72	0.32	0.65	0.03	0.80	0.18	0.66
Part-time (day) FE	-0.34	0.28	0.12	0.49	-0.06	0.50	-0.01	0.37
Years of service	0.71	0.63	0.63	-0.36	0.74	0.09	0.71	-0.14
Income			0.34	0.09				
Manual worker's income			–	–	-0.31	0.01	-0.32	0.04
Company status			-0.64	-0.27	–	–		
Security: top manager			0.34	-0.12	–	–		
Use of abilities			0.31	0.01	–	–		
Security expectations					0.41	0.01	0.42	-0.05
Society unionateness							-0.24	-0.52
Relative contribution of functions: per cent	58	42	62	38	62	38	56	44
Group centroids: co-ordinates								
Member of neither	-0.63	-0.14	-0.20	0.62	-0.51	0.44	-0.39	0.59
Mild trade union	0.40	0.66	0.97	-0.00	0.82	0.36	0.90	0.24
Trade union	0.16	-0.26	-0.20	-0.25	-0.03	-0.28	-0.10	-0.31
Correctly predicted: per cent								
Member of neither	50		62		53		59	
Mild trade union	57		69		69		62	
Trade union	52		57		54		59	
Total	52		60		56		60	

Including factors associated with social location brings about a moderate improvement in overall prediction (to 60 per cent). The effects of the educational variables and of years of service are much the same as before, but we now find also that those earning more and those who believe their jobs are more demanding and more secure incline more towards the mild unions. The only factor which clearly predisposes towards membership of full trade unions is perceived company status, but contrary to what we might expect it is those with higher perceptions, other things being equal, who are involved in trade unions. It seems quite likely that this effect, which in any case disappears when other factors are introduced, is reflecting a difference between central and local government. In local government each establishment covered the whole range up to the most senior jobs, whereas our central government establishments were regional offices with few senior officials who, in any event, probably thought in terms of their status within the national department.

Introduction of expectations, satisfactions and outcomes adds nothing to the overall success of predictions. (Indeed without outcomes it declines, a good example of the SPSS handbook's warning that 'the result is only optimal (rather than maximal) because not every possible subset is considered' (Nie *et al.*, 1975, p. 448).) However the inclusion of society unionateness, which obviously best discriminates the full union members, does lead to a more even balance of correct predictions for each category. The two elements of further education remain significant as, even more, does the number of years of service, and their effect remains in general much the same. The factors relating to social location cease to be significant. Two new factors, though, are expectations of security – highest amongst those who tend towards the mild trade unions – and perceptions of the earnings of an average manual worker – higher amongst the non-members.

An approach to differences in the nature and extent of membership between the public sector and the private is to use the methods that are adopted in considering the effect of availability in Chapter 4. Taking just those groups in private employment for whom either a union or a staff association is available in order to make the situations more comparable, we can carry out a discriminant analysis of membership of either kind of body. The discriminating variables obtained, appropriately weighted, can then be applied to those employed in the public sector as a means of estimating expected membership – that is as if similar processes operated as in private employment. Because of possible feedback effects from involvement, we have carried out the

analysis both including and excluding enterprise and society unionateness. We have already seen that there are such effects in the private
sector, and we shall shortly be considering their significance for the
publicly employed. In fact inclusion of the two unionateness measures
does not affect the general pattern of results although it does tend to
soften all the contrasts, for reasons that we shall consider later. We shall
therefore simply present these alternative results in parentheses. Table
6.3 compares the sectors for the three membership categories, giving the
percentage of predicted to actual size of each and the percentage of
correct predictions.

Naturally, the overall proportion of correct predictions is lower for
the public sector, than for those on whom the analysis was originally
carried out. However, what are more interesting are the differences in
the correct predictions for each membership category. In particular
there is a marked difference for full union members: where the private
sector analysis gives a success rate of 67 (73) per cent, there is a fall to just
26 (39) per cent for public employees. The reason for this is, as we might
anticipate, the large under-estimate of union membership in the public
sector. There are considerable discrepancies between the actual and
predicted proportions in the three membership categories, but even
these mask substantial differences between occupational groups. Most
notably, the predicted percentage of managers and professionals in a full
trade union is less than 1 per cent, compared with an actual figure of 49
per cent, so that the proportion of predicted to actual membership is just
over 1 per cent. This rises to 25 per cent (i.e. four times as many actual as
predicted) when the unionateness measures are included – a dramatic
improvement but still a large discrepancy.

TABLE 6.3 *Comparison between public and private sectors of actual membership
as against that predicted by the discriminant functions for the private sector*
(percentages)

	Public		Private	
	Predicted/ actual membership	*Correctly predicted*	*Predicted/ actual membership*	*Correctly predicted*
Nothing	172(145)	53(59)	51(68)	35(55)
Mild organisation	204(200)	66(68)	208(185)	64(60)
Full trade union	34(48)	26(39)	156(132)	67(73)
All		40(49)		48(61)

Figures in parentheses are when unionateness is included.

The figures for clerks, technicians and others are obviously higher as they must offset their very low estimates, but there is still a considerable under-estimate of union membership, the predicted proportion being only 55 (63) per cent of the actual, For these groups the predicted percentage of non-members is very close to the actual, although this does not mean that successful prediction of individual non-members is very high. However the largest predicted category in their case is that of mild trade union members, and the over-estimate is considerable – 323 (278) per cent. This result is particularly interesting when we bear in mind that in the private sector staff associations were the more likely form of representation in situations of large numbers of non-manual workers, and relatively few manual. On the other hand, it is worth noting that membership of staff associations also tends to be over-estimated in the private sector, by about two-to-one.

The proportion of managers and professionals in a mild trade union is also overestimated by this method, though less dramatically – 133 (153) per cent. They are most likely to be allocated to the non-member group – 62 (47) per cent of them are placed there, as against 23 per cent who actually belong.

The general picture, then, is that using the results from the private sector to predict the situation for public employees is relatively unsuccessful. Full trade union membership is considerably under-estimated on this basis, while mild union membership, particularly in the case of the lower-status occupations, and non-membership in the case of managers and professionals are overestimated. It is not that member-ship cannot be predicted in the public sector: there are differences between non-members and members of the two types of union and the separate analysis (Table 6.2) gave a comparable level of correct prediction to that attained in the private sector. The point is that the criteria are different and less stringent in identifying full union members. Even though we have used only those groups in the private sector for whom representation is available, it is clear that the propensity to be members of representative bodies, especially full trade unions, among public employees is much greater than among the privately employed. However these results largely confirm what we have already noted, serving mainly to demonstrate that the previous results cannot be accounted for by differences in individual characteristics and work experience.

A more important question that remains is whether membership of either major kind of representative body has the same meaning in the public as in the private sector. Since prediction of membership is substantially improved by the inclusion of society and enterprise unionateness the relations involving them are obviously similar in the two areas of employment, but the extent of that similarity is unclear. Thus we need to consider in more detail the relations between involvement and both enterprise and society unionateness.

In looking at those in private employment we noted (Table 2.7) a general pattern in which enterprise unionateness rose with greater involvement in both trade unions and staff associations, while society unionateness tended to rise in the former case, but fall in the latter. Much the same is true for those in the public sector, with the significant difference that society unionateness does not actually decline at higher levels of involvement in mild trade unions. Nonetheless members of the two types of organisation do differ in this regard, particularly at the higher occupational levels. As we have said, the mild trade unions are chosen mainly by those, apart from clerks, in central government, where such bodies predominate. Similar groups in local government choose full trade unions. Although there are no significant differences in enterprise unionateness between members of the mild unions in central government and of the full trade unions in local government, they do differ markedly in society unionateness, with the latter scoring significantly higher ($E = 0.45$ for managers and professionals, $E = 0.39$ when technicians and draughtsmen are included). Thus experience of a more unionate body seems to modify the attitudes of these higher-status groups. By contrast, clerks share similar levels of unionateness whatever the character of the representative body of which they are members.

When a direct comparison is made between members of the different kinds of bodies in the public and private sectors one interesting point is that amongst trade union members, who are by far the largest group in each case and the most comparable, there is little difference in the average level of enterprise unionateness ($E = 0.03$). In that sense, therefore, the individual commitment to collective bargaining, given union membership, seems as strong in the public as in the private sector, and since there are proportionately many more members in the former case, much stronger overall. This is so despite the greater proportion of members who are from higher-status occupations and in fact, as we saw in the previous volume, there is little variation by occupational level in enterprise unionateness in the public sector. Moreover members of the mild trade unions score significantly higher than do members of staff associations, particularly at the higher-status levels (managers and professionals, $E = 0.32$; the remainder, $E = 0.24$).

When we turn to society unionateness the distinction between mild trade unions and staff associations is maintained for both of the broad occupational groupings. That is to say, it is higher amongst members in the public sector ($E = 0.24$ for both groups, though this is significant only at the 10 per cent level for managers and professionals). Thus, even though it may be the case that, for some groups especially, the milder trade unions exist as a means of matching the lower unionateness of their potential members, this is much less true than it is of staff associations for private employees. Among full trade union members, however, society unionateness is significantly higher in the private sector ($E = 0.21$), as we would anticipate given the greater membership among higher-status groups in the public sector, coupled with the fact that even there these groups score lower on society unionateness. In fact though, this difference is not simply a result of the larger proportion of high-level occupations in public sector unions. Within each occupational group, public employees in full trade unions exhibit lower levels of society unionateness than do their private sector counterparts, with the most significant differences being for clerks and technicians ($E = 0.23$ in both cases). Disaggregating the society unionateness measure into its component items reveals that whereas, overall, public employees are more likely to agree that most people need representation, to prefer trade unions to company-based bodies and to prefer unions to be registered, they are no more likely to agree with TUC affiliation and less likely to agree with affiliation to the Labour Party. To what extent this reflects simply an unwillingness on the part of public servants to identify their representative organisations with a particular political party (even indirectly through the TUC) is difficult to say, but it seems unlikely that this would account for all of the difference. The conclusion seems to be that commitment to the wider labour movement amongst union members is lower in the public sector.

On the other hand we should not lose sight of the fact of the much greater involvement in the public sector. The determinants of society unionateness lie to a large extent outside immediate work experience and the extension of membership to groups and individuals who outside public employment would have a lower propensity to join is almost certain, even given some feedback effect from involvement, to reduce the mean level. The main question is whether such a feedback effect operates in the public sector, and if so how it compares with the private.

To examine these issues further we use analysis of variance and associated multiple classification analysis. Our main interest is in differences between the three categories of membership (none, staff association/mild trade union, and full trade union) and in looking at these we take account of broad occupational category (managers and professionals against the rest). In some analyses we also included, as factors or covariates, a number of individual characteristics which are important determinants of unionateness, so that we could take account of their effect as well. Of particular relevance, of course, is the sector of employment, which we treat in two ways by conducting both separate analyses for each sector to investigate interaction effects and joint analyses, where the sector is itself a variable.

The most direct use of the analysis is through the beta coefficients, which are a form of partial correlation between unionateness and each of the variables with control for the rest. However we can also make use of estimated means for different groups which also serve to illustrate what is involved. The estimate for each group is the mean value that would obtain if the influence of the variables concerned were uniform for all groups. In Table 6.4 we present, for society and enterprise unionateness, estimated means derived from analyses of (a) both sectors jointly and (b) each separately (in all cases excluding individual characteristics). Together with these are included actual means, providing a basis for comparison and also a summary illustration of the earlier discussions.

Still considering society unionateness, the first point to note is that there is no independent effect from sector of employment, regardless of whether the analysis includes individual characteristics (beta = 0.02 with them and 0.03 without). Thus being employed in the public sector in itself neither adds to nor subtracts from commitment to the labour movement. This is reflected in the joint estimates (a) in the table, where we can see that for each category of membership and occupational group the figure for public employees is close to, though slightly below, that of those in private employment. The major differences in the joint analysis, as may be seen from the estimated means, are between occupational groups (beta = 0.11) and especially types of membership (beta = 0.41). With allowance for individual characteristics the relation of society unionateness to occupation almost disappears, while that with membership category is not much affected (beta = 0.03 and 0.38 respectively). This is in keeping with a substantial feedback effect, from membership to unionateness, as already observed for the private sector.

However, there is also a significant effect from the interaction of employment sector and type of membership, i.e. the relation between membership and level of society unionateness is different in the two sectors. We can get a good idea of the nature of this interaction by looking at the estimates (b) for each sector separately. Although in both

TABLE 6.4 *Actual and expected means of society and enterprise unionateness by membership category, occupational grouping and sector of employment*

| Occupational status | Society | | | | Enterprise | | | |
| | Lower | | Higher | | Lower | | Higher | |
Sector	Public	Private	Public	Private	Public	Private	Public	Private
Membership								
Non-member								
Actual	14.6	14.2	12.9	13.4	28.2	22.5	28.2	15.2
Estimated (a)	14.0	14.3	13.1	13.3	27.5	21.9	23.1	17.5
(b)	14.7	14.2	13.5	13.4	28.5	22.1	28.8	16.3
Staff association/mild union								
Actual	15.6	13.6	13.4	11.3	35.1	28.9	34.7	25.1
Estimated (a)	13.7	14.0	12.8	13.1	35.8	30.2	31.5	25.7
(b)	14.6	13.4	13.5	12.6	35.1	29.0	35.4	23.3
Trade union								
Actual	16.5	17.7	15.9	16.0	36.5	35.5	36.9	32.9
Estimated (a)	17.2	17.5	16.3	16.6	40.7	35.1	36.2	30.7
(b)	16.7	17.8	15.6	17.0	36.5	36.4	36.8	30.6

(a) joint analysis, including both sectors.
(b) separate analyses by sector.

cases there are significant differences between the categories of membership, they are less marked in the public sector (beta = 0.30) than in the private (beta = 0.42). This reflects mainly the fact that full trade union membership does not entail as strong a commitment to the labour movement in the former case – which tends to confirm earlier results. The estimated means from the separate analyses are notably lower for trade union members in the public sector, and close to the actual values. However it is also true that membership of a mild trade union does not involve so negative a view of the labour movement as does membership of a staff association. In fact comparison with the actual means shows that this is especially true for the lower occupational groups. The actual value in their case is well above the estimated, while that for their higher-level counterparts is a little below. In the case of staff associations in the private sector there is a similar tendency, although here the lower-status groups score only a little above the estimated value, while managers and professionals score a good deal below. The two categories with marked differences show up even more clearly in the joint analysis.

We have been concentrating on membership but the analyses do, of course, take equal account of occupational level. Without allowing for membership category the overall difference between the occupational groups is much the same in each sector (beta = 0.20 public and 0.19 private). However, when allowance is made the difference is then greater for public (beta = 0.17) than for private employees (beta = 0.10).

There can be little doubt, then, that while commitment to the wider labour movement, as indicated by our measure of society unionateness, is greater overall in the public sector, the consequences of union membership are not as clear as they are in private employment. This is true for the lower-status occupational groups as well as for the higher and, except to a very minor extent, cannot be accounted for by differences in social background and experience. These results cannot be interpreted simply as indicating that membership has less effect on attitudes in the public sector. The circumstances leading to the different patterns of membership may themselves involve different views of the labour movement. In this connection it is noteworthy that, as indicated by responses to the separate items, the lower society unionateness scores are largely attributable to a lower level of agreement with the 'stronger' items referring to affiliation to the TUC and the Labour Party. Nonetheless, the tendency should not be exaggerated. It is worth noting that outright opposition appears less marked – even the small number of non-members in higher-level occupations do not have as low a score as similar groups in private industry who are members of a staff association. As we have said, when the different proportions who are members are considered it is remarkable that the tendency is not much greater, and a question mark inevitably remains hanging over the issue of the extent to which identification with a particular political party is seen as a practical problem with respect to central or local government employees.

Another possibility is that public employees tend to identify the institutions of the labour movement with sectional rather than general interests, that is with the particular interests of manual workers. We have suggested that the traditional theories about general interests (class) – which identify common interests with common circumstances as wage labourers in a system of commodity production – offer inaccurate statements of economic processes and as a consequence provide no adequate basis for common organisation. If institutions are too closely identified with such partial understandings of experience, their relation to collective interests will be limited. However there has been for some years a growing tendency for white-collar unions to affiliate to the TUC. This has continued since the data of this study were collected, with an increasing number of members from the public sector, and it seems likely that the TUC is evolving into a body which includes understandings and actions which are less explicitly 'capitalist'.

Enterprise unionateness is far less problematic and the further analysis, including the results shown in Table 6.4, essentially confirms previous findings. The difference between the two sectors of employment is significant (beta = 0.13), even when account is taken of the relevant characteristics of employees in them (beta = 0.12). It is clear from the table that managers and professionals differ most between the two sectors. Thus for this group in the public sector the estimates in the joint analysis are in all three instances below the actual values, most notably in the case of non-members, while in the private sector they are above, with the exception of union members. For lower-status occupations the estimates from the joint analysis are reasonably close to the actual, except in the case of union members in public employment, who are considerably below their estimated value. As we could anticipate from this result, while differences between membership categories are significant both in the joint and the separate analyses, the effect is weaker in the public sector (beta = 0.25, as against 0.36 for both the private sector and the joint analyses). This suggests that as with society unionateness there is less feedback effect from union membership, although we should again stress the much more extensive unionisation in terms both of full trade union membership and the more unionate character, compared with staff associations, of the mild trade unions.

In the private sector, the managers and professionals are significantly distinguished from the other occupational groups. They thus tend to differ from their counterparts in public employment, and there is no doubt that a fuller analysis of the latter would be highly desirable. In particular, the question of the consequences of unionisation of this group merit further study. Unfortunately, the issues involved when one begins to make comparisons are complex ones and are beyond the scope of this present work. However the evidence on the face of it suggests two things. The first is that, allowing for qualifications, education, age and other personal and job characteristics, professional and managerial employees in the public sector are better paid than their private sector counterparts. The reverse is the case for all other occupational groups. How far this is a result of the generally rather different kinds of occupations at these levels in the public sector is difficult to determine without further analysis.

The same is true for the other point indicated by our evidence. This is that there is a markedly stronger relation between respondents' occupations and those of their fathers among this higher-level group in public employment than among any other sub-group. Without a considerably more detailed analysis of the occupations involved in the two cases it is difficult to know whether this is a genuine result or, if it is, what are the processes that have brought it about. Data from the Oxford Mobility Project confirm the continuing superior ability of the more advantaged to secure education and qualifications for their children (Halsey, Heath and Ridge, 1980). They also suggest a slight tendency for these children to be better able to attain the professional and technical occupations for which such qualifications are relevant than the administrative and managerial occupations in Classes I and II (Goldthorpe, 1980: figs 5.1–5.3 and 5.11–5.14. We suspect that narrower definitions of both occupational groupings and classes would show the relation more clearly). Thus the explanation may well lie in the greater bureaucratisation of the public sector and the greater preponderance of occupations requiring formal qualifications.

More, generally, of course, it can be convincingly argued that the more advantaged groups in society derive greater relative benefit from the provision of most public resources (Le Grand, 1981). The apparent basis of their advantage in the operation of market forces is now taken as a commonplace, but these same forces were at one time seen by writers as diverse as Marx and Marshall as having an egalitarian influence on earnings. Thus it is important to bear in mind that similar processes of the reproduction of inequality may well distort the operation of the alternative, non-market criteria that we have emphasised, in directions quite different from those that are suggested by their potentiality.

7 Conclusions

In Chapter 1 we stated that our purpose was to analyse the relations between class location and experience and involvement in collective representation. Those in the classical Marxist tradition had no doubts about the nature of such relationships, that trade unions were a reflection of the inevitable conflict of interest between the employer, representing capital, and employed workers, but the collecting together of all the latter into the proletariat has limited the usefulness of this theoretical approach in analysing, for example, the differential distribution of union membership. Instead, a 'sociological tradition' in the area of white-collar unionisation has attempted to combine elements of Marx with a more refined definition of class situation. The perceived necessity for some adaptation of the traditional theory also lies behind a more recent Marxist approach. In this the basic division between classes is maintained, but a 'middle' class is in effect introduced by subterfuge, by means of the concept of 'contradictory class locations'. Certain groups, it is argued, share in the functions both of capital and of labour (or provide only labour-power within the capitalist function) and thus cannot be uniquely allocated to one or the other class (Carchedi, 1977; Wright, 1978, 1979). Moreover, 'the heterogeneous and ambiguous nature of the white-collar class situation is reflected in heterogeneous and often contradictory forms of collective representation' (Crompton, 1976). This last writer explicitly accepts that 'as far as it goes' the sociological approach to unionisation in relation to class situation is a satisfactory one. Within the same limits, therefore, it may well appear that the results that we have presented, at least as regards the private sector, are consistent with the theoretical position she represents. Thus, to see why we reject that position it is necessary to look at what is proposed beyond the limits.

Crompton's argument is that the sociological approach falls down by failing to account for changing class situations. These, she believes, can be explained only 'by explicit reference to the development of the capitalist mode of production'. However, while we welcome and agree with the necessity for such attempts to locate traditional sociological

143

theories of class action within a broader theoretical framework, we are doubtful of the fruitfulness of concentrating on the capitalist mode of production, given the previously recognised need to modify the Marxist position. The concept of the capitalist mode of production belongs within a theory that also provides a statement of its development. It is inconsistent (if not contradictory) to add the idea of contradictory class locations to a theory which contains within one of its central concepts a very different idea of contradiction. The result of such a revision is, as Holmwood and Stewart (1981) argue, that 'the explanations adduced are inconsistent with the theory of proletarianisation as a theory of the polarisation of classes since they shift the emphasis from a statement of contradictory class locations resolved in proletarianisation to a state-ment of contradictory class locations maintained in the contradictory nature of "proletarianisation" as a process'. In developing their critique these writers show how close this position is at heart to that of the neo-Weberians, including those using the 'sociological approach', whom they criticise. In both cases there is an attempt to separate the economic from the social, and an ultimate resort to a voluntarism in which 'the "individual" becomes the means whereby this or that principle operates in the empirical world'.

A second ground for our rejection of this modified Marxist position relates to Wright's arguments concerning the returns to positions associated with exercising part of the function of capital. These are based on the one hand upon a particular (probably authentic) view of the nature of surplus value and its distribution, and on the other upon a separation of individuals and positions. As we have shown elsewhere (Stewart *et al.*, 1980, ch. 10) the evidence he brings forward to support his position can be accounted for quite differently and more satisfactorily.

The other failing of these and other Marxist theories, which is more directly relevant to this present work, is in their treatment of the public sector. The development of the state is seen as 'a characteristic feature of the development of monopoly capitalism', and the main concern of the state is 'with the distribution of surplus value which is acquired through different forms of taxation and levies' (Crompton, 1976, p. 426). However, it is not at all clear how the concept of surplus value is being used in this and similar statements. Since a large part of the revenue is derived from taxes, direct and indirect, levied upon labour, it can hardly refer to that part of value appropriated by capital. A usage more faithful to Marx is to regard it as value created which is in excess of the reproduction costs of labour-power, but this raises several inter-related problems. In general terms these centre around the role of the market. Since the reproduction costs of labour-power are determined by market forces, all activities carried on by the state, the results of which are distributed on non-market criteria, are defined out of the area of production (in fact this is a corollary of regarding them as paid for out of surplus value). Apart from the odd consequence that in different societies various activities will be differently categorised according to whether or not they are provided on a market basis, such a view reinforces a bourgeois conception of a distinction between economic needs, served by the market, and social needs served, to the extent that they can be 'afforded', by the state. Not only do we find this theoretically unsatisfactory, we find it difficult to reconcile with a Marxist conception of an increasingly all-pervasive capitalist mode of production. Indeed, any idea of such social needs would seem to be rather close to Marx's view of a future society in which it would be necessary to deduct from the total social product ('the co-operative proceeds of labour', not 'surplus value'), amongst other things, (a) 'that which is intended for the common satisfaction of needs, such as schools, health services etc.' which, it should be noted, 'grows considerably in comparison with present society and it grows in proportion as the new society develops', and (b) 'funds for those unable to work' (Marx, n. d.).

It is the existence of substantial public provision on the basis of non-market criteria, that is those other than individual ability to pay, which makes it unfruitful to apply in any simple way the concept of the capitalist mode of production. Thus issues of class cannot be treated basically in terms of relationship to the means of production, whether simply or by the use of the idea of contradictory class locations. We believe that it is important to look at processes of socially structured advantage and disadvantage, the ways in which these are reproduced and changed, and the consequences in terms of experience for groups differently located within the processes. In Western societies this must mean taking account of the 'market', for which the ideology claims an objective existence outside the social, a distinct 'economic' realm, by means of which is legitimated both a particular role for capital as a 'factor of production' and a set of principles for distribution.

We deny the validity of such attempts to divorce the economic from the social. Any 'market' operates, more or less well in its own terms, only within a given set of social conditions. The neo-Weberian approach tends to see this point only in so far as it implies 'distortion' of an otherwise free market, and it concentrates on class action which is orientated towards market position. As we argued in Chapter 1, it is possible to advance a different view of class action, as that which is concerned with pursuing alternative principles of distribution. This we did in order to counter those who claimed that there was no necessary relation at all between class and collective representation.

Whilst we accepted that class consciousness, in the sense of proletarian identification, was neither a necessary nor a sufficient condition for collective representation, we had argued in our previous volume that individual and group action should be seen in the context of their relation to class processes – that is, those of socially structured advantage and disadvantage. As well as showing the significance of the trade union movement for class action, in the sense of changing current processes in a more egalitarian and universalistic direction, we also believed that we would find, in the British context, a strong relation between collective representation and class in the sense of relative disadvantage under current processes. That is, among the non-manual workers with whom this study is concerned, we anticipated that the development of collective representation in the form of trade unions would occur in those situations and among those groups where relative disadvantage was most marked. Such trade unions would have a character similar to those for manual workers, but we did not expect that they would necessarily be identical, because of the different situations of the occupational groups that they represented. Similarly, we recognised that there would be some forms of collective representation whose class nature would be very much weaker. Partly this would be reflected in the enterprise unionateness of such organisations, that is in the purely industrial militancy and methods used in pursuing their aims, but more importantly in their society unionateness, the extent of their identification with the wider labour movement.

Our results for the private sector, covering a wide range of situations, provide very clear evidence of the relationship between trade unionism and class experience. Although there are minor differences according to whether one looks at individual involvement or the pattern of availability for different occupational groups, the overall picture is quite clear. Trade unionism tends to be concentrated among those filling the lower-level occupations in the non-manual hierarchy which are less well paid and generally less highly rewarded. However, what is important is the relation of positions of that kind to the career processes of which they form a part. Some may be filled by younger men who are likely to move into better positions; more significant for unionisation are those filled by older men who have experienced other types of routine work. Thus we find that in many cases it is one or other element of education or qualifications which is related to union involvement, with the less well qualified being more likely to be members and so on. Similarly, the level of the individual's first job or his starting position in his present company often emerges as the more important factor.

In considering the unionisation of non-manual workers, therefore, it is a mistake to view them statically, as a single group or a number of occupational sub-groups. Rather, it is necessary to look at the occupations in terms of the kinds of individuals typically carrying them out. Then it becomes clearer that union involvement does not simply depend upon current experience, although this is important, but upon the present in relation to past, and anticipated future, experience. Unionisation is more likely amongst those whose situation within the non-manual hierarchy is least advantageous and offers least opportunity for personal competence, but to a large extent it is the case that such positions are filled by individuals with close personal experience of, or family links to, manual work.

As the analysis was extended beyond the individual level to take in the contextual features of the employing establishment, so the existence of connections between non-manual unionism and the manual working class, of a slightly different kind, became more significant. First, it appeared to be the case that workers with the characteristics, and filling the kinds of positions, that we have been describing tend to be concentrated in particular types of establishments, those that are larger, marked by a greater degree of specialisation in administrative functions, and more likely to be externally controlled. These are also establishments in which large numbers of manual workers are employed and where, in consequence, collective negotiations for the latter are well established. The existence of such negotiations and the influence that they seem to have on management's general attitude towards collective bargaining, in particular their willingness to extend recognition to trade unions, is a major factor in stimulating the development of similar machinery for groups of non-manual workers. In much the same way the fact that unionism tends to be stronger in larger communities indicates the importance of a demonstration effect, or of a general climate of opinion favourable towards trade unionism.

This aspect, of climate of opinion, emerges elsewhere, in relation to the importance of society unionateness. Although we have no directly comparable data it is probably correct to say that non-manual employees, even those agreeing with representation and perhaps being union members, are less favourably disposed towards militant collective action than manual workers. Equally, they may not show the same degree of support for the wider labour movement, in terms of affiliation to the TUC or the Labour Party. Nevertheless, such support, as indicated by society unionateness, is a major determinant of trade union involvement, and the higher the level of involvement the greater is the commitment to the labour movement.

However, as we have said, we did not expect to find that all forms of representation for non-manual workers would show the same clear relationship to class experience. Indeed staff associations, which were the only other form that was of sufficient significance to be dealt with, are most clearly separated from trade unions by the low degree of society unionateness in terms both of their own character and of the pre-dispositions of their members. With regard to their individual characteristics those involved in staff associations are not, in fact, completely distinct from those involved in trade unions. They tend also to be in lower-level positions, with lower status and income, and to be older (or of longer service in the company). However in terms of their schooling and their work experience (first job and first job in their present company) there is less evidence of contact with manual workers. More are likely to have started in a non-manual job, and consequently to exhibit less apparent career movement. Thus the less 'class conscious' nature of staff associations is explicable in part by the more limited experience of those for whom that kind of representation is more likely to develop. Again it became clear from the analysis of establishments that we are dealing with situations in which numbers of individuals with similar characteristics are concentrated in certain kinds of firms. Further, the nature of these situations where particular types of employee are gathered together is very different from those conducive to trade unionism. In particular, there is again a lack of close connection with manual workers. Staff associations develop where there are large numbers of non-manual workers, but few manual. As with trade unions, they are encouraged by a more bureaucratic form of organisation, particularly as this is reflected in the degree of specialisation.

Despite the existence of two rather different forms of representation there is a high degree of consistency in the private sector. Personal experience of and wider contacts with manual work are important for both forms of organisation. Where experience and contacts are most developed trade unionism is the usual type of collective representation, expressing as it does both militancy for the groups covered and identification with the wider labour movement. Where contacts with manual workers are lacking representation is more likely to occur through staff associations, which express slightly less militancy and markedly less identification with the labour movement, perhaps even antipathy towards it.

There can be little doubt, then, of the relationship of collective representation to occupational location and 'class' experience as far as the private sector is concerned. What, though, of public employment? The obvious facts of the very much more highly developed system of collective bargaining for public employees, and the much higher rates of membership in trade unions, suggest that quite different principles operate. It is difficult to believe that experience which accentuates common interest with manual workers of the kind we have found to be important in the private sector is so much more extensive in public employment, particularly as it would have to extend to higher-level groups such as professionals and administrators. Indeed, given that the circumstances of employment of most non-manual workers in the public sector are more akin to those of the kinds of employees in the private sector who become involved in staff associations, we could reasonably expect that it would be organisations of that type which would be most likely to develop.

It is true that we did find in the public sector some trade unions, catering particularly for the higher-level occupational groups, which have a resemblance to staff associations. Equally, it was the case that at any occupational level society unionateness was lower among members of trade unions in the public sector than in the private. Thus there are certainly grounds for arguing that the substantial growth of collective bargaining for public employees is not straightforwardly 'class'-related in the sense of widespread identification with the labour movement. On the other hand, a majority of the trade unions are not of what we called the mild variety, akin to staff associations. Moreover, given that such a high proportion at all occupational levels are members of one or other kind of representative body, it could be argued that what is surprising is that such identification should be as developed as it is. Even those in mild trade unions, with the possible exception of managers and professionals, show higher levels of society unionateness than do their staff association counterparts. Part of the reason for this is that, as we saw in the previous volume, in the public sector higher enterprise unionateness tends to lead to higher society unionateness. Another is strongly suggested by our results from the private sector, where we found that involvement in a trade union similarly tends to increase identification with the wider labour movement. Since, in public as in private employment, it is the managers and professionals who are most sharply distinguished from the remainder, it is highly likely that such influences operate quite strongly at the lower occupational levels.

Our evidence, then, shows that, doubts regarding professionals and managers apart, trade unions and their members in the public sector differ in degree rather than in kind from those in the private sector. As we argued earlier, the class-related nature of the latter is quite clear. What may still appear strange is the widespread adoption of collective bargaining for those in public employment and the relation that it bears to class experience. Clearly this relationship is not the same as in the private sector. In order to understand the connection between the two, and thus how they can result in a unified labour movement, it is necessary to appreciate that each represents different aspects of a single process. This process is the one that we began to discuss in the concluding chapter of the previous volume and elaborated in certain respects in the introduction to this one. It is the substitution of what are, or appear to be, market criteria of allocation by other, more universalistic criteria. As we argued previously, the question of the application of market principles is central to class relations. In the private sector class experience leads to trade unionism which, albeit in a limited way, questions the application of such principles and attempts, at least in part, to supplant them. One, relatively advanced, aspect of such questioning would be the advocacy of public ownership of the company or industry concerned (cf. Banks, 1970).

This last point provides the clue to the link with the public sector, for here market principles are clearly more attenuated, if they apply at all. This is perhaps least true for undertakings under public control which are closely involved with the private sector, often formerly under private ownership, but even here it has proved very difficult for quite determined governments to have them run on 'normal commercial lines'. This is so whether the undertaking is an unsuccessful 'lame duck' or one which is 'too successful'. However in areas which are more distant from the private sector, particularly where a product or service is publicly provided rather than privately purchased, the attenuation of market principles is more pronounced. It affects not only the distribution of what is produced or provided but also, because the one is dependent upon the other, the determination of the price of labour used. Hence the need for 'comparability' with the 'market-determined' sector as a means of deciding salary levels.

Capitalism as a system, whether in conservative or Marxist perspectives, is organised around market principles, and class relations are centred on the operation of these principles. In a 'pure' form capitalism has never existed but, for reasons too complex for our present analyses, understandings of a capitalist form have served, more or less efficiently, in the reproduction of social life. They have had to be amplified by *ad hoc* treatments of specific difficulties (such as wage determination in the public sector) and there have been various attempts to subsume non-capitalist entities under the umbrella of capitalist forms (e.g. the corporate state and the new middle class), but the limited nature of capitalism as a statement of modern social and economic forms and so of the organisation of efficient behaviour is becoming increasingly obvious. The development of the public sector represents an important deviation from capitalist principles and, as we argued in the first chapter, a major element in that development came about as a result of the activity of the labour movement. In terms of practical (and theoretical) understanding the public sector both challenges and sets problems for market principles of distribution. It is the main area in which the production of social resources occurs and these, as we have argued, cannot be assimilated to the market. It is likely that the shifts in understanding that are involved as this area grows in significance will occur most readily amongst those with the closest practical experience – public employees. This, together with an element of self-interest, would ensure a greater degree of sympathy than might otherwise be anticipated with the broader aims of the labour movement in the general provision of resources. At the same time, as we have said, employment relations take on a different class character because they are no longer tied so closely to market principles. Instead, other, more bureaucratic and more universalistic criteria are applied, of the sort that elsewhere would be the object of trade union action. Thus, trade unions in the public sector are not so much reactions to a continuing class situation, but more a reflection of an already-modified class relationship. That is, there is a consonance between the employment situation, no longer bound by an ideology of market principles, and collective representation.

This situation also generates its own problems; the public sector is the one most clearly subject to attempts by the government to manage the economy through income or employment policy. However the desire of the government to manage incomes and employment is part of a general departure from market principles. Public sector employees may be particularly exposed to government action, but incomes policies are general in their intentions and attempt to set controls other than 'what the market will bear'.

The link that we argue, then, is between trade unions in the private sector, reflecting the particular interests of their members and pursuing alternative principles to those of the market, and those in the public sector which reflect the operation of such alternatives and hence a transformation of class relationships. Of course we are aware that in neither case is the process extensively developed. The concept of the market, dominating economic and, ultimately, social arrangements, is a very powerful one. There is no doubt that the understanding and the actions of trade unionists and others in both the private and public sectors is still substantially influenced by it. The organisation of the labour movement still reflects such an understanding to a marked degree. Since it is a limited understanding which reflects the interests of certain types of employee more than of others, it may in part explain the disinclination of our white-collar employees (especially those in the public sector) and their representative organisations to ally themselves too closely to that movement. However, since the time of our study a number of public sector trade unions have joined the TUC, though not the Labour Party, and this may involve a change in the nature of priorities within the labour movement.

Our own view is that practical developments, like the rise of the public sector, will continue to throw up problems for current capitalist understandings and so transform them as, equally, practical arrangements will be transformed. Our evidence, we believe, suggests that non-manual unions will play a full part in this process.

Appendix
Interview Schedules
and Checklist

(a) INDIVIDUAL INTERVIEW SCHEDULE (items dealing with representation only)

(Questions 1–32, see Appendix I of Prandy, Stewart and Blackburn, 1982, and the discussion, *passim*, of the constructed measures.)
[Q. 32. Statements: 'People like me need, on our behalf . . . .'

A 'no kind of collective representation'
B 'a representative body to consult with and advise the employers on salaries and conditions'
C 'a representative body to negotiate with the employers'
D 'a representative body to negotiate, which is prepared, if necessary, to take mild industrial action'
E 'a representative body to negotiate which is prepared, if necessary, to take full strike action'

Scores for compatible orderings: ABCDE (0), BACDE (11), BCADE (17), BCDAE (26), BCDEA (31), CBDEA (32), CDBEA (43), DCBEA (47), DCEBA (51), DECBA (57) and EDCBA (66).]

If he agrees only with statement (a) 'no representation': ask Q. 35 next.

33. Do you know of any type of representative body – trade union, staff committee, professional association and so on – that would be appropriate for the activity(s) that you have agreed with?
   If none: ask Q. 34.
   Otherwise:
   (i) Which is the most appropriate?
   Name

   (a) Are you currently a member of (this body)?
      If no: ask Q. (b).

If yes: ask Q. (c).

(b) Have you ever been a member?

If yes: Did you leave because of any disagreement with policy? Are you seriously considering (re-)joining? *Miss Q. (d)–(f)*

(c) Do you intend to remain a member?

(d) Do you hold any local or national office in (this body)?

If no: Have you ever held any local or national office?

(e) About how many meetings have you attended in the past year?

(f) Do you discuss (this body's) affairs at work:

very often; often; sometimes; rarely?

(g) Would you say that in carrying out its activities (this body) has been:

very successful; half and half; fairly unsuccessful; very unsuccessful?

(ii) Are there any others that would be appropriate or of which you are in fact a member?

34. Thinking more generally, what type of representative body would you most like to carry out the activities with which you agreed

(a) Firstly, would you prefer it to be a body
(i) solely for employees of this company, or
(ii) for employees only in this industry, or
(iii) covering employees in several industries?

(b) Secondly, would you prefer it to be a body
(i) only for people with the same occupation as your own, or
(ii) only for occupations at about the same level, or
(iii) for all grades of non-manual employees, or
(iv) for both manual and non-manual employees?

35. Are you eligible for membership, or studentship, of any qualifying or professional associations?

If yes: Which of the following do you think is the most important activity for a professional association?

Granting qualifications

Education and study

Professional protection (i.e. concerned with salaries and status)

What is the next most important?

If professional protection is not mentioned, ask:

Do you think that a professional association should concern itself with protecting salaries and status?

(b) INDIVIDUAL CHECK-LIST (representation items only)

(Sections I–VII, see Prandy, Stewart and Blackburn, 1982.)

SECTION VIII

Finally, we should like to know your general attitude towards representation (through consultative machinery, staff associations, trade unions, etc.).

Could you tick the appropriate box to indicate how much you agree or disagree with each statement.

This company is very fair to its employees.
This company does not really like its staff to join a trade union.
This company's products or services are very desirable and useful.
Top management in this company has no understanding of our problems.
Membership of a trade union would seriously harm my promotion prospects.
Most people need some sort of organisation to protect their interest with regard to their employment.
In my case, good communications make formal representation unnecessary.
I would prefer to be in an internal company association rather than a trade union.
I would prefer to be in a registered trade union.
I would prefer to be in an organisation affiliated to the TUC rather than one not affiliated.
I would prefer to be in an organisation affiliated to the Labour Party rather than one not affiliated.

THANK YOU VERY MUCH INDEED FOR YOUR CO-OPERATION

(c) EMPLOYER INTERVIEW

Name of employing organisation

1. Is this establishment part of a larger group?
   If yes:

What is the total number of employees within the group (i.e. the ultimate owning group)?

2. (a) What is the total number of employees within this establishment?
   (b) What was the total number of employees within this establishment in 1964?
   (c) Could we have a breakdown of your establishment by the following occupational categories? (Male; female; total)

   (a) Manual workers
   (b) Foremen
   (c) Clerical workers
   (d) Draughtsmen
   (e) Technicians
   (f) Scientists, technologists and other professionals
   (g) Managers
   Total non-manual

3. Do you have any system of grading non-manual employees within the establishment? If so, could we please have a breakdown of the numbers in each grade?

4. Is there a person whose sole responsibility (i.e. does not have other responsibilities) is carrying out one or part of one of these activites?

   Obtaining and controlling materials and equipment (e.g. buying, material control, stores and stock control).

   Carrying outputs and resources from place to place (e.g. transport, driving, despatch, transport administration).

   Recording and controlling financial resources (e.g. accounts, costs, wages).

   Maintaining and erecting building equipment (e.g. maintenance, works engineer).

   Controlling the quality of materials, equipment and outputs (e.g. inspection, testing).

   Maintaining human resources and promoting their identification with the organisation (e.g. welfare, medical, safety, magazine, sports and social).

   Controlling workflow (e.g. planning, progressing).

   Disposing of, distributing and servicing the output (e.g. sales and service, customer complaints).

   Acquiring and allocating human resources (e.g. recruitment, selection).

   Devising new outputs, equipment and processes (e.g. research and/or development, drawing office).

Assessing and devising ways of producing the output (e.g. work study, operations research, rate fixing, methods study).

Developing and operating administrative procedures (e.g. organisation and methods, registry, filing and statistics).

Developing and transforming human resources (e.g. education and training).

Developing, legitimising and symbolising the organisation's charter (e.g. public relations, advertising).

Acquiring information on the operational field (e.g. market research, specialised economic analysis).

5. What is the highest level at which assent *must* be obtained before action is taken on each of the items below (even if others have subsequently to confirm the decision)? The categories are follows:

5   Above chief executive
4   Chief executive (i.e. for the establishment)
3   Departmental managers immediately responsible to the chief executive
2   Other departmental managers and equivalent level
1   Supervisors
0   Operators (including clerical, technical workers etc.)

Labour force requirements
Appointments to direct worker jobs
Promotion of direct workers
Representing the organisation in labour disputes
Number of supervisors
Appointment of supervisory staff team outside the establishment
Promotion of supervisory staff
Salaries of supervisory staff
To spend unbudgeted or unallocated money on capital items
To spend unbudgeted or unallocated money on revenue items
What type, or what brand, new equipment is to be
Overtime to be worked
Delivery dates or priority of orders
To determine a new product or service
To determine marketing territories covered
The extent and type of market to be aimed for
What costing system shall be applied
What shall be inspected
What operations shall be work studied
Plans to be worked on

Outputs to be scheduled against given plan
Dismissal of operative
Dismissal of supervisor
Methods of personnel selection
Training methods to be used
Buying procedures
Which suppliers of materials are to be used
Methods of work to be used (not involving expenditure) i.e. how a job is to be done
Machinery or equipment to be used for a job
Allocation of work among available workers
What and how many welfare facilities are to be provided
The price of the output
To alter responsibilities/area of work of line departments
To create a new department
To create a new job
Who takes over in chief executive's absence

6. Is your company a member of an employers' association?
7. Do salary negotiations take place

   (a) within this establishment?
   (b) within the company?
   (c) nationally?

8. About what proportion of your manual workers are covered by agreements negotiated

   (a) within this establishment?
   (b) within the company (or group)?
   (c) nationally?

9. (a) Could you please give some idea as to general company policy on the question of representation of employees? The set of statements below cover a wide variety of views that employees might have about representation. What do you think the company would consider to be the appropriate form of representation, if any, for each of the categories in the table below? We want to know the company's ideal, not what actually happens.

   A No kind of collective representation.
   B A representative body to consult with and advise the employers on salaries and conditions.
   C A representative body to negotiate with the employers.

D A representative body to negotiate, which is prepared if necessary, to take mild industrial action.

E A representative body to negotiate, which is prepared if necessary, to take full strike action.

(b) In those cases where you have suggested some form of representation, which form of grouping do you think the company would prefer this representation to be based on?

N.B. Please distinguish between internal (company-based) bodies, e.g. a staff committee, and external ones.

10. Could you please supply the following financial information with respect to this establishment or, if this is not possible, to the next largest accounting unit.

(a) Sales turnover:
- (a) 1968–9
- (b) 1967–8
- (c) 1963–4
- (d) 1962–3 (or percentage change 1962–4 to 1967–9).

(b) Earnings data:
Gross wage and salary bill (total).

(c) Assets: Net: i.e.
- (a) fixed assets net of accumulated depreciation;
- (b) plus total current assets;
- (c) less total current liabilities.

(d) Income:
(Gross trading profit).

(d) REPRESENTATION INTERVIEW

We should be grateful if you could let us have the following information regarding your membership. This will be treated as STRICTLY CONFIDENTIAL. If you are not sure about the occupational categories, this can be cleared up at the interview. (Male; female; total)

(a) Foremen
(b) Clerical workers
(c) Draughtsmen
(d) Technicians
(e) Scientists, technologists and other professionals
(f) Managers
Total

Could you also tell us how many meetings there have been in the past year which could have been attended by members in this establishment?

Number of official (i.e. branch etc.) meetings.
Number of social meetings.

Bibliography

Ahrne, G., U. Himmelstrand and L. Lundberg (1978) '"Middle Way" Sweden at a Cross-Road: Problems, Actors and Outcomes', *Acta Sociologica*, vol. 21, no. 4.

Bain, G. S. (1967) *Trade Union Growth and Recognition* (Royal Commission on Trade Unions and Employers' Associations, Research Paper No. 6) (London: HMSO).

Bain, G. S. (1970) *The Growth of White-Collar Unionism* (Oxford University Press).

Bain, G. S., D. Coates and V. Ellis (1973) *Social Stratification and Trade Unionism* (London: Heinemann).

Bain, G. S. and R. Price (1972) 'Union Growth and Employment Trends in the United Kingdom, 1964–1970', *British Journal of Industrial Relations*, vol. 10, no. 3.

Banks, J. A. (1970) *Marxist Sociology in Action* (London: Faber & Faber).

Blackburn, R. M. (1967) *Union Character and Social Class* (London: Batsford).

Blackburn, R. M. and M. Mann (1979) *The Working Class in the Labour Market* (London: Macmillan).

Braverman, H. (1974) *Labor and Monopoly Capital* (New York: Monthly Review Press).

Burkitt, B. (1975) *Trade Unions and Wages* (Bradford University Press).

Butler, D. and D. Stokes (1969) *Political Change in Britain* (London: Macmillan).

Carchedi, G. (1977) *On the Economic Identification of Social Classes* (London: Routledge & Kegan Paul).

Crewe, I., B. Sarlvik and J. Alt (1977) 'Partisan Dealignment in Britain', *British Journal of Political Science*, vol. 7, no. 2.

Crompton, R. (1976) 'Approaches to the Study of White-Collar Trade Unionism', *Sociology*, vol. 10, no. 3.

Crompton, R. and J. Gubbay (1977) *Economy and Class Structure* (London: Macmillan).

Doeringer, P. B. and M. J. Piore (1971) *Internal Labor Markets and Manpower Analysis* (Lexington, Mass.: D. C. Heath).

Dunleavy, P. (1980a) 'The Political Implications of Sectoral Cleavages and the Growth of State Employment: Part 1, The Analysis of Production Cleavages', *Political Studies*, vol. xxviii, no. 3.

Dunleavy, P. (1980b) 'The Political Implications of Sectoral Cleavages and the Growth of State Employment: Part 2, Cleavage Structures and Political Alignment', *Political Studies*, vol. xxviii, no. 4.

Elliott, R. F. and J. L. Fallick (1981) *Pay in the Public Sector* (London: Macmillan).

Flanders, A. (1970) *Management and Unions* (London: Faber & Faber).

Fogel, W. and D. Lewin (1974) 'Wage Determination in the Public Sector', *Industrial and Labor Relations Review*, vol. 27.

Fox, A. (1975) 'Collective Bargaining, Flanders, and the Webbs', *British Journal of Industrial Relations*, vol. XIII, no. 2.

Gallie, D. (1978) *In Search of the New Working Class* (Cambridge University Press).

Giddens, A. (1973) *The Class Structure of the Advanced Societies* (London: Hutchinson).

Glyn, A. and R. Sutcliffe (1972) *British Capitalism, Workers and the Profits Squeeze* (Harmondsworth: Penguin).

Goldthorpe, J. H. (1980) *Social Mobility and Class Structure in Modern Britain* (Oxford University Press).

Halsey, A. H., A. F. Heath and J. M. Ridge (1980) *Origins and Destinations* (Oxford University Press).

Hewitt, C. (1977) 'The Effect of Political Democracy and Social Democracy on Equality in Industrial Societies: A Cross-National Comparison', *American Journal of Sociology*, vol. 42, no. 3.

Hicks, A., R. Friedland and E. Johnson (1978) 'Class Power and State Policy: The Case of Large Business Corporations, Labor Unions and Governmental Redistribution in the American States', *American Journal of Sociology*, vol. 43, no. 3.

Holmwood, J. M. and A. Stewart (1981) 'The Role of Contradiction in Modern Theories of Social Stratification', mimeo.

King, J. E. (1972) *Labour Economics* (London: Macmillan).

Korpi, W. (1978) 'Social Democracy in Welfare Capitalism – Structural Erosion, Welfare Backlash and Incorporation' *Acta Sociologica Supplement*.

Le Grand, J. (1981) *The Strategy of Equality* (London: Allen & Unwin).

Lewis, H. G. (1963) *Unionism and Relative Wages in the United States: An Empirical Enquiry* (Chicago University Press).

Lockwood, D. (1958) *The Blackcoated Worker* (London: George Allen & Unwin).

Mann, M. (1973) *Consciousness and Action among the Western Working Class* (London: Macmillan).

Marx, K. (n.d.) *Critique of the Gotha Programme* (Moscow: Foreign Languages Publishing House).

Mulvey, C. (1978) *The Economic Analysis of Trade Unionism* (Oxford: Martin Robertson).

Nie, N. H., C. H. Hull, J. G. Jenkins, K. Steinbrenner and D. H. Bent (1975) *SPSS: Statistical Package for the Social Sciences* (New York: McGraw-Hill).

Parkin, F. (1979) *Marxism and Class Theory: A Bourgeois Critique* (London: Tavistock).

Peters, B. G. (1974) 'Income Distribution: A Longitudinal Analysis of France, Sweden and the United Kingdom', *Political Studies*, vol. XXII, no. 3.

Poulantzas, N. (1973) *Political Power and Social Classes* (London: New Left Books).

Prandy, K. (1965) *Professional Employees* (London: Faber & Faber).

Prandy, K. (1979) 'Alienation and Interests in the Analysis of Social Cognitions', *British Journal of Sociology*, vol. XXX, no. 4.

Prandy, K., A. Stewart and R. M. Blackburn (1974) 'Concepts and Measures: The Example of Unionateness', *Sociology*, vol. 8, no. 3.

Prandy, K., A. Stewart and R. M. Blackburn (1982) *White-Collar Work* (London: Macmillan).

Pugh, D. S., D. J. Hickson, C. R. Hinings and C. Turner (1968) 'Dimensions of Organisation Structure', *Administrative Science Quarterly*, vol. 13, no. 1.

Reddaway, B. (1959) 'Wage Flexibility and the Distribution of Labour', *Lloyd's Bank Review*, 54.

Roberts, B. C., R. Loveridge and J. Gennard (1972) *Reluctant Militants: A Study of Industrial Technicians* (London: Heinemann).

Routh, G. (1980) *Occupation and Pay in Great Britain 1906–79* (London: Macmillan).

Stephens, J. D. (1979) *The Transition from Capitalism to Socialism* (London: Macmillan).

Stewart, A., K. Prandy and R. M. Blackburn (1980) *Social Stratification and Occupations* (London: Macmillan).

Turner, H. A. (1957) 'Inflation and Wage Differentials in Great Britain', in J. T. Dunlop (ed.), *The Theory of Wage Determination* (London: Macmillan).

Wilkinson, R. K. (1962) 'Differences in Earnings and Changes in the Distribution of Manpower in the United Kingdom, 1948–57', *Yorkshire Bulletin of Economic and Social Research*, vol. 14, no. 1.

Wright, E. O. (1976) 'Class Boundaries in Advanced Capitalist Societies', *New Left Review*, vol. 98.

Wright, E. O. (1978) *Class, Crisis and the State* (London: New Left Books).

Wright, E. O. (1979) *Class Structure and Income Determination* (New York: Academic Press).

Index